WORLD WAR II
BATTLE OF BRITAIN

WORLD WAR II
BATTLE OF BRITAIN

Published by Bookmart Ltd 2005

Blaby Road,
Wigson,
Leicester,
LE18 4SE
Books@bookmart.co.uk

All notations of errors or omissions (author inquiries, permissions) concerning the content of this book should be addressed to TAJ Books 27, Ferndown Gardens, Cobham, Surrey, UK, KT11 2BH, info@tajbooks.com.

ISBN 1-84509-169-8

Printed in China.
1 2 3 4 5 08 07 06 05

Contents

UK Home Front anti-aircraft guns in London.

As in the days of Philip of Spain, Louis XIV, and Napoleon, Britain's chances of resisting an invasion from the Continent depended on retaining control of the Channel and the North Sea.

For an attack on Britain in 1940, Hitler was considerably weaker than Napoleon had been in 1805. The heavy naval losses suffered in the Norwegian campaign had reduced the German fleet to the strength of one pocket-battleship, four cruisers, and a dozen destroyers. But the enormous superiority of the British Home Fleet, based on Scapa Flow, was countered by the numerical strength of the Luftwaffe, plus the danger represented by U-boats and torpedo-boats. This triple threat would have made

Home Fleet operations in the Narrow Seas far too hazardous, and the Admiralty, in the light of the experience of Dunkirk, was unwilling to risk the fleet further south than the Wash.

Thus the Channel and the southern approaches to the North Sea became a sort of naval no-man's-land. In the skies above these waters victory or defeat for the Luftwaffe would decide whether or not Germany risked an invasion attempt.

Britain's weaknesses after Dunkirk

Would a defeat for the R.A.F. have permitted the Wehrmacht to land — as envisaged by the O.K.H. Directive of July 27, 1940 — on the coasts of Kent, Sussex, the Isle of Wight, and Dorset? At the time of the French armistice at Rethondes on June 22, the British Army in Britain totalled some 26 divisions, of which 12 had been formed recently and were not yet fully trained or equipped. The 13–14 divisions which had seen action in France had lost most of their artillery and antitank weapons, and had brought back only 25 out of their 600 tanks. Nor had the troops been assigned equal sectors of the south coast to defend. Around Brighton, Montgomery's 3rd Division had some 30 miles of coastline to watch; between western Sussex and Wales, Sir Alan Brooke's Southern Command consisted of a corps staff and a mere three divisions, of which two were Territorial.

On June 26, Brooke wrote gloomily: "The main impression I had was that the Command had a long way to go to be put on a war footing … The more I see of conditions at home, the more bewildered I am as to what has been going on in this country since the war started. It is now ten months, and yet the shortage of trained men and equipment is appalling … There are masses of men in uniform, but they are mostly untrained: why, I cannot think after ten months of war. The ghastly part of it is that I feel certain that we can only have a few more weeks before the boche attacks."

This was hardly an exaggeration. On July 19 General Ironside, C.-in-C., Home Forces, had been relieved of his post. Although he was promoted to field-marshal and given a seat in the House of Lords, this was still seen as a disgrace, since it was only two months since he had been replaced as Chief of the Imperial General Staff by General Sir John Dill. But was Ironside alone responsible for the weaknesses of the British Army? In his memoirs, Eden says not. He refers to the "surprising bitterness" with which Dill criticised Hore-Belisha, former Secretary of State for War. "He had done damage to the army that could not be repaired in years, Dill said, commanders had come to look over their shoulders."

Passing Southern Command to General Auchinleck, who had done so well at Narvik, Brooke took over from Ironside and threw himself into intense and timely activity as commander of the Home Forces. Making lavish use of aircraft transport, he was everywhere, countermanding the strict defensive prescribed to all sectors and releasing mobile reserves for counterattacks. But this was not enough: he also had to order that the areas in which such counter-attacks might have to be made were cleared for action, by demolishing the concrete obstacles which had studded village streets since May.

Brooke's responsibilities were far greater than the resources at his disposal. In the diary which he kept for his wife, he occasionally gave vent to the anguish which the immediate future caused him. On September 15 he wrote:

"Still no move on the part of the Germans. Everything remains keyed up for an early invasion, and the air war goes on unabated. This coming week must remain a critical one, and it is hard to see how Hitler can retrace his steps and stop the invasion. The suspense of waiting is very trying, especially when one is familiar with the weaknesses of one's defences. Our exposed coast line is just twice the length of the front that we and the French were holding in France with about eighty divisions and the Maginot Line. Here we have twenty-two divisions of which only about half can be looked upon as in any way fit for any form of mobile operations. Thank God the spirit is now good and the defeatist opinions expressed after Dunkirk are no longer prevalent. But I wish I could have six months more to finish equipping and training the forces under my command. A responsibility such as that of the defence of this country- under existing conditions is one that weighs on one like a ton of bricks, and it is hard at times to retain the hopeful and confident exterior which is so essential to retain the confidence of those under one and to guard against their having any doubts as regards final success."

The organisation responsible for the defence of the island was not likely to soothe Brooke's worries. If the Germans had tried an invasion they would have encountered no inter-service high command capable of co-ordinating the efforts of the British Army, Navy, and Air Force. The First Sea Lord had no less than six "commanders-in-chief" under his orders, while the Chief of the

Air Staff had three. And Brooke had no authority to give orders to any of them.

"This system," he wrote after the war, "presented grave dangers. If a landing had taken place I fear that Churchill, as Minister of Defence, would have tried to co-ordinate the activity of the different commands himself. This would have been a perilous mistake, for with his impulsive nature he would have tended to take decisions according to his intuition and not from a logical perspective."

It was no less urgent to replace the matériel lost at Dunkirk as soon as possible, to raise the divisions still training to battle-worthiness, and to arm the Home Guard, which in August 1940 contained one million volunteers. To this end, guns were taken from military museums and war memorials; the Drury Lane Theatre contributed a dozen rusty old rifles; shotguns and ammunition were commandeered; and even cutlasses from the navy of Nelson's day were distributed to the local defence volunteers.

Stepping up production

Meanwhile, the arms factories were accelerating their production all the time. On June 8 there were 72 infantry and cruiser tanks in Britain; this rose to 200 by August, and there were 438 by September 29. The production rate was expected to rise to 12–15 per week for infantry tanks and nine per week for cruiser tanks. But these tanks, although brand new, were — as Rommel was to prove in Libya — already obsolescent for modern armoured warfare.

Britain took over from France the military contracts which the latter had signed with the United States and which had not been completed by the time of the armistice. But, most important of all, Roosevelt agreed to provide Britain with 500,000 rifles and 900 75-mm guns, each supplied with 1,000 shells. By the "cash and carry" principle still in force, the British Merchant Navy was responsible for bringing these precious cargoes home, and this was done with no losses to U-boat attacks. Churchill commented that certain generals turned up their noses at these 900 guns, which dated from the end of World War I. But the British were desperately short of artillery: on June 8 there were only 420 field guns and 163 heavy guns, with 200 and 150 rounds per gun respectively. And during the second phase of the Battle of France the 75-mm gun had proved its worth as a tank-killer. On June 8 the British Home Forces had only 54 2-pounder (40-mm) guns which could be used against tanks.

By September 17 Brooke had the following resources for the defence of Great Britain and Northern Ireland: 29 divisions and eight independent brigades, six of which were armoured. These forces included two Canadian divisions, the 1st and 2nd, of which only the 1st Division had suffered at all (one man killed and five missing) during its recent excursion to France. This little army, faced with invasion, was outnumbered by an estimated four to one — and on top of that it was still not ideally deployed.

Raeder prepares for a Channel crossing …

During the winter of 1939–40, not wishing to be caught unprepared by a sudden demand from Hitler, Grand-Admiral

Raeder had ordered his staff to make a study of the many problems which would have to be settled if he were ordered to transport the German Army across the Channel.

On May 21, 1940, at the moment when the Panzers were driving onwards from Abbeville towards Boulogne and Calais, Raeder told Hitler of the conclusions reached by these studies. But the information fell upon preoccupied ears. As late as June 20 Raeder had still received no reaction from Hitler on the subject: when he made his report and asked for instructions, all he got from the Führer were some vague suggestions for a scheme to transport Jews to Madagascar.

... and Hitler dallies

Hitler's indifference to Raeder's invasion suggestions on May 21 was not surprising: his attention was focussed on the battle in hand. He was apprehensive that the temerity of his generals would allow the French to stage a new "Miracle of the Marne", recovering as they had done in 1914. Later, on the eve of the arrival of the French armistice delegates at Rethondes, Hitler's dilatory attitude towards Raeder was the result of his uncertainty about the best road to take now that France had been crushed. At Munich on the 18th, Ciano had seen Hitler as an actor preparing to play the part of Charlemagne, "the gambler who has made a big scoop and would like to get up from the table risking nothing more", and wondering if there were any real advantage in overthrowing the awesome mass of the British Empire. Would Churchill see sense? Would he fall? Either of the two would make an invasion of England unnecessary.

London air raid shelter is open day and night.

From June 25 to July 5 Hitler remained with a small group of consultants aboard his special train Tannenberg at Kniebis, near Freudenstadt in the Black Forest, waiting for the situation to become clarified one way or the other. On July 2 a landing in England was certainly the object of an order-but it was only a hypothetical case, together with several others, and no preparations were to be made yet.

It was on July 16, in Berlin, that Hitler signed his famous Directive No: 16 — Seelöwe (Operation "Sea Lion"). But the preamble to this document shows that even at this date the invasion was not regarded as inevitable. It stated: "Since England, in spite of her apparently hopeless military situation, shows no sign of coming to terms, I have decided to prepare a landing operation against England, and if necessary to carry it out.

"The aim of this operation is to eliminate the British homeland as a base for the further prosecution of the war against Germany, and, if necessary, to occupy it completely."

This was not, therefore, Hitler's final word. But a month had passed since the fall of Paul Reynaud's government and France's request for an armistice, and those 30 days had not been wasted by the British aircraft industry, ably stimulated by Lord Beaverbrook. Allowing for two more months of preparations and preliminary moves, an invasion would not be possible until September 16 — on the eve of the period of boisterous early autumn weather which would make the Channel impassable to light landing-craft.

From the Reichstag on July 19 Hitler addressed an ultimatum, dressed up as an offer of peace, to Winston Churchill. Churchill was recommended, in all conscience, to make the British people see reason, for he, Hitler, could see no reason for the struggle to continue. He would not be responsible for any further shedding of blood. London made no reply to this insolent harangue; and Hitler was forced to go ahead with the build-up for "Sea Lion". On July 27 Brauchitsch — recently promoted to Field-Marshal, together with 12 other Army and Luftwaffe generals — submitted a preliminary invasion plan to O.K.W. With 41 divisions, six of them armoured and three motorised, plus the Luftwaffe's 7th Parachute Division and the 22nd Airborne Division.

As the man responsible for the land forces during the assault crossing, and for their supply during the campaign, Raeder denounced the whole ambitious scheme as impracticable. Even by requisitioning every available vessel from the inland waterways and the fishing fleets — which would have serious results on war production and civilian food supplies — he would not be able to assure the landing of a first wave of 13 divisions, even if their numbers were considerably reduced. The Navy also condemned the idea of a landing on the wide front envisaged by Brauchitsch, stating that adequate protection could not be guaranteed and recommending a crossing in the Pas-de-Calais sector. But Brauchitsch and Halder in turn refused to consider feeding troops into the narrow Ramsgate-Folkestone sector suggested by Raeder and his chief-of-staff, Admiral Schniewind.

The result was a compromise. The 6th Army venture from Cherbourg was dropped completely, and O.K.H. agreed to concentrate its right flank between Ramsgate and Folkestone. But the plan for 9th Army remained unchanged, and Rundstedt would still have a sufficiently wide front for his break-out. This adjustment lowered the invasion force to 27 divisions, nine of them in the first wave, each of which would land 6,700 men on D-Day, now set for September 21. A feint landing against the Norfolk coast was also planned, to draw off the British reserves from immediately behind the landing beaches.

As there was no German battle fleet to give heavy gunfire support, and as the Luftwaffe would be unable to provide total coverage for the assault, it was decided to give the landing troops the benefit of tank fire-power. To do this, some 128 Pzkw III and IV tanks were converted to allow them to be landed offshore and descend to the seabed, a depth of 25–30 feet below the surface. Because of the extra 0.8 atmospheres pressure created at this depth, careful waterproofing was needed: the turret ring of each tank was sealed with an inflatable tube; and the crew and the engine got their air supply via a long, flexible snorkel tube supported on the surface, while a special valve coped with the exhaust problem. Special landing-craft with hinged ramps, and their bottoms reinforced with concrete to bear the weight of the tanks, would carry the tanks to their launch points off the British coast.

Experiments carried out by Reinhardt's XLI Panzer Corps off the island of Sylt in the North Sea proved that these submarine tanks were perfectly capable of carrying out this task. Finally, long-range artillery support was provided by coastal batteries which could reach the British coast between Ramsgate and Dungeness: four batteries between Sangatte and the north of Boulogne, with four 28-cm, three 30.5cm, four 38-cm, and three 40.6-cm guns, with ranges of between 28 and 37 miles.

The point of balance

Was the Battle of Britain lost before it began? Or did Hitler and Göring fail to make a thorough and methodical use of their advantages?

On August 13, 1940 — Adlertag, the "Day of the Eagle"-the losses of the Battle of France had not yet been recouped by the Luftwaffe. (The French Air Force alone had caused the loss of 778 German aircraft.) To tackle England, the Luftwaffe was deployed in three air fleets:

Norway and Denmark: Luftflotte V (Stumpff);

Ground crew bomb-up a Stuka for a night raid on England.

Belgium. and Holland: Luftflotte II (Kesselring); and Northern France: Luftflotte III (Sperrle). On August 13 the Luftwaffe deployed 2,422 aircraft against Britain: 969 bombers, 336 Ju 87 dive-bombers, 869 Bf 109 single-engined fighters and 268 twin-engined Bf 110 "destroyer" fighters.

The British, however, had come a long way since the days of the "Phoney War". Fighter production — 157 in January 1940, 325 in May, 446 in June, and 496 in July — was no longer .a serious worry. The supply of trained pilots was far more serious. On July 13 Fighter Command, led by Air Chief-Marshal Sir Hugh Dowding, had only 1,341 trained pilots; it would have to draw heavily upon the pilots of Coastal Command and the Fleet

German HE IIIH bomber over London.

could climb faster than the British fighters; the British fighters were more manoeuvrable, and their batteries of eight machine guns gave them a bigger, though lighter, cone of fire that the German fighters.

Two paramount elements favoured the R.A.F. First was the defence radar network extending from the Shetland Islands to Land's End At the western extremity of Cornwall. Radar information enabled the British commanders to get their fighters off in sufficient time to avoid attack on the ground and then, directed over the radio, to intercept the enemy, often surprising him.

Second came the fact that Fighter Command was operation largely over British soil and could recover most of its shotdown pilots. German aircraft shot down over Britain almost always meant the loss of their crews as well as their machines. On August 15, for example, the R.A.F. destroyed 70 German fighters and bombers. Some 28 Spitfires and Hurricanes were shot down that day — but half their pilots eventually rejoined their squadrons.

Air Arm, as well as forming four Polish and one Czech squadron in a few weeks.

This meant, on the surface, that this decisive battle would pit 1,137 German fighters against 620 R.A.F. Hurricanes and Spitfires-but the comparison is not as simple as that. The Messerschmitt Bf 110 twin-engined "destroyer" fighter"Göring's folly"-was too slow and too sluggish to hold its own against the British fighters. On the other hand the Messerschmitt Bf 109E single-seat fighter was faster than the Hawker Hurricane Mk. I and about as fast as the Supermarine Spitfire Mks. I and II, although the latter machine had only begun to appear with the front-line squadrons of R.A.F. Fighter Command. The Bf 109

1st Phase: Attacks on shipping and coastal ports (July 10 to August 7). German fighter tactics prove definitely superior, while the British Defiant turret-fighter is shown to be useless. The British concentrate on raising pilot strength and building up for the battle ahead. Losses: Fighter Command 169; Luftwaffe: 192 (+77 damaged).

2nd Phase: Attacks on radar stations and forward fighter bases (August 8 to 23). The climax of this phase occurs, on August 15. Attacks from Scandinavia are repulsed with heavy losses, but in the south Fighter Command suffers heavy losses and pilots begin to show signs of extreme fatigue. Göring spares the R.A.F. by deciding to abandon attacks on radar stations. Losses: Fighter Command 303; Luftwaffe 403 (+127 damaged).

3rd Phase: Attacks on aircraft production and inland fighter bases (August 24 to September 6) with strong fighter escort to tempt British fighters up. The Bf 110 and Stuka have proved easy meat for the Spitfires and Hurricanes, but British pilot losses and fatigue have reached desperately high levels. Losses: Fighter Command 262; Luftwaffe: 378 (+115 damaged).

4th Phase: Attacks on London (September 7 to 30) in a final effort to destroy British air power after the realisation that Fighter Command is still a force to be reckoned with. Battle reaches climax on the 15th. "Sea Lion" postponed in definitely, and Germans switch tactics to high-level fighter-bomber raids. Losses: Fighter Command: 380; Luftwaffe: 435 (+161 damaged).

5th Phase: The aftermath (October 1 to 31). German fighter-bomber sweeps and preparation for the Blitz. Fighter Command reserves in aircraft and pilots increase rapidly. Losses: Fighter Command 265; Luftwaffe 325 (+163 damaged).

For some 25 years the accepted idea has been that the German air offensive reached its peak on Sunday, September 15; during a series of German attacks on London, the British defence claimed to have shot down 185 German aircraft, a total lowered to 56 by the official post-war figures. In fact, although the British came close to defeat on the 15th they had already won, as much because of the mistakes of the German high command as the courage of the R.A.F. fighter pilots. The Luftwaffe's offensive had begun badly: in five days of operations between August 13 and August 17, the Germans lost 255 aircraft to the R.A.F.'s 184. As a result Göring withdrew Luftflotte V and the Stuka formations from the battle — Luftflotte V because it was badly placed to make worthwhile attacks on targets in northern England, and the Stukas

Squadron of DC-215s on their way to London.

UK bombing damage - German bomber brought down on London Victoria Station

as opposed to 262 British planes shot down or destroyed on the ground. On paper this suggests that the R.A.F. still had an advantage of 45 per cent — but in fact these figures were far more favourable to the Luftwaffe than might be imagined, because the German losses were shared between the fighters and the bombers. On the British side the brunt fell on Fighter Command, now reduced to under 1,000 pilots, constantly in action and desperately in need of rest.

With casualties of 15 to 20 pilots killed and wounded every day, Fighter Command was nearing its last gasp when suddenly the whole picture changed.

Turning-point: the London Blitz

Late in the evening of August 24, a German bomber formation accidentally bombed some non-military targets in London. Churchill's immediate response was to order a reprisal raid on Berlin. The following night, 81 twin-engined bombers took off for the German capital, but only 29 reached Berlin; the others got lost on the way. This modest raid cost the British eight men killed and 28 wounded-but this time it was Hitler's turn to lose control. Forgetting that he had formerly regarded "terror bombing" as a dangerous distraction from the main effort, he immediately ordered that London be given the same treatment as Warsaw and Rotterdam. On September 7 the first heavy "Blitz" raid broke on London, with some 330 tons of bombs being dropped.

The bombing of London continued for 57 consecutive nights — but it meant that Hitler and Göring had abandoned the principal objective of the directive of August 1. The Luftwaffe

because they were too vulnerable.

However, as long as the Luftwaffe kept up its attacks on the Fighter Command bases in southern England it was close to winning set and match. Many British aircraft were destroyed on the ground, and their essential runways riddled with bomb craters. Far more serious, however, was the fact that the operations centres, unfortunately sited on the airfields themselves and insufficiently protected against bombs, suffered heavy damage, which caused additional difficulties in co-ordinating the formations in the air.

During this phase — August 24 to September 6 — the scales tilted heavily in favour of the Luftwaffe, which lost 378 aircraft was unable to smother London with terror raids without relaxing the grinding pressure which it had been inflicting on the British fighters. Fighter Command recovered rapidly: between September 7 and September 30 the British gained the upper hand over the Luftwaffe, destroying some 380 aircraft for a loss of 178 of their own.

By October 31 the Luftwaffe had lost 1,733 fighters and bombers to the R.A.F.'s 1,379 fighters — but the R.A.F. had lost only 414 pilots killed (of whom 44 were Allied, mainly Poles). Churchill, therefore, was not exaggerating when he proclaimed the R.A.F.'s victory in the House of Commons with the immortal sentence: "Never in the field of human conflict has so much been owed by so many to so few." The same praise was repeated when he wrote after 1945. But at the time he was far less satisfied with the results obtained. The brilliant C.-in-C., Fighter Command, Air Chief-Marshal Sir Hugh Dowding, and the commander of Fighter Command's No. 11 Group, Air Vice-Marshal Keith Park, the real brains behind the victory, were deprived of their commands within weeks and relegated to secondary posts. The ostensible reason was that there had been far too many faults in the field of radio communications and that the battle had been fought too much on the defensive, using "pennypacket" tactics.

Air Chief-Marshal Sir Hugh Dowding has by far the strongest claim to being the victor of the Battle of Britain. Before World War II he spared no effort in building up Fighter Command into the magnificent weapon which it was in the vital summer of 1940. He stoutly resisted the demand to fling Britain's last reserve of fighter squadrons into the Battle of France, and so preserved the

London air raid scene wreckage from enemy bombs.

metropolitan fighter force which met and defeated the German attempt to gain day and night control of the air over Britain.

The invasion postponed

Across the Channel the final preparations for Operation "Sea Lion" were being pushed ahead at an uneven pace. On shore, the troops of 16th and 9th Armies were concentrated around their embarkation points. At sea, however, the mine-laying and mine-sweeping programme intended to secure the invasion lanes from British attacks had suffered badly from attacks by Coastal Command — and Göring had failed to smash the R.A.F. Against the German invasion fleet — 2,500 transports, barges, tugs,

Scene from the cockpit of a Luftwaffe bomber over burning England.

lighters, and light craft massed in the invasion ports between Rotterdam and Le Havre — R.A.F. Bomber Command was intensifying its attacks. True, the losses of the invasion fleet were under ten per cent, but they still had to be replaced.

On September 11 Hitler announced his intention of beginning the count-down for "Sea Lion" on the 14th, which would place the landing at dawn on Tuesday, September 24. But on the 14th he decided to take three more days to decide whether or not to give the final order.

In 1940, September 27 was the last day in which the tides were favourable for such a venture. From then on into October, the high seas and strong winds which could be expected in the Channel would be too much for the inland craft to risk the crossing; they would have stood a good chance of foundering. On the 17th, Hitler ordered "Sea Lion" to be postponed. Two days later he gave the order for the invasion fleet to be dispersed in order to protect it from British bombing, but in such a way that it could be readily reassembled as soon as he needed it.

But the real implications ran far deeper. On October 12, while the ravages of the German Blitz were being extended across England, Keitel issued the following order from O.K.W.:

"The Führer has decided that until next spring the preparations for Seelöwe are to be continued with the sole intention of maintaining political and military pressure on Britain …

"Should the projected landing be resumed in spring or early summer, orders will be given for new preparations. In the meantime, it is necessary to shape conditions in the military sphere to suit a final invasion."

Still in the ring

By autumn 1940 all neutral powers and the occupied countries knew that the Anglo-German struggle had not ended, and that this fight to the death would not be resumed until spring. What would happen then? On July 15 Weygand had said to Colonel P. A. Bourget, who had followed him from Beirut to Bordeaux; "although British victory is still not certain, neither is that of Germany". If Weygand was talking in this fashion only 20 days after the signing of the armistice, it is easy to imagine the tremendous encouragement given three months later to the early resistance networks forming in France, Belgium, and Holland by the postponement of "Sea Lion". Now the defeat of May–June 1940 had been proved to be provisional; Hell had become Purgatory; cruel sufferings lay ahead, but they would not last for ever …

German Luftwaffe BF109 crashed in field with British soldier in cockpit.

Greek soldiers leaving for the Albanian front.

first glimmer of hope since June 25,1940. From the moment the attack began, Mussolini and Ciano watched while the political assumptions on which the war with Greece had been founded began to collapse. They already knew that King Boris of Bulgaria would stay on the sidelines until events had run their course. They had grossly underestimated the patriotism of the Greek nation, which closed its ranks under the feeble Italian bombing raids when it heard that King George II and the Prime Minister, General Joannis Metaxas, had indignantly rejected the Italian ultimatum and had immediately decreed general mobilisation.

The fact was that Italy was violently unpopular in Greece. Quite apart from the historical legacy of the Venetian rule in Crete, the Morea, and the Ionian Islands, the Fascist methods brought to bear on the people of Rhodes and the Dodecanese by Count Cesare de Vecchi had resulted in the unanimous hostility of all sectors of Greek opinion against Mussolini, his régime, and his country.

Hitler had hardly left Montoire after his uncomfortable meeting with Pétain when a message from the German Ambassador in Rome threw him into the deepest consternation: his ally was on the brink of invading Greece. In the hope of staving off this dangerous venture, he went straight to Italy instead of returning to Berlin. At 1000 hours on October 28, he was greeted at the station in Florence by Mussolini, all smiles: "Führer, we are on the march! At dawn this morning our Italian troops victoriously crossed the Albanian-Greek frontier!"

Koritsa, Taranto, and Sidi Barrani were three decisive defeats for Italian arms which severely darkened the prospects of the Axis. They gave the suppressed peoples of Western Europe their

The Greeks hit back

General mobilisation gave the Greek commander, General Alexandros Papagos, 15 infantry divisions, four infantry brigades, and a cavalry division, formed into five army corps. On paper the Greek divisions were definitely inferior to the Italian divisions, but this disparity was largely balanced by the chronic difficulties of the terrain and of communications, which favoured the defenders.

In the Italian plan the initial assault would be carried out by four divisions attacking in Epirus, with another two divisions covering the main attack by advancing against the Morova massif.

Visconti-Prasca planned a breakthrough which would surprise Papagos before he could concentrate his forces. But the weather was on the side of the Greeks: the Italians crossed the frontier in torrential rain which converted every brook into a torrent and every road into a sea of clinging mud. In these conditions the demolitions carried out by the Greeks added still further to the slowing-up of the Italian advance.

Nevertheless, Visconti-Prasca's left-hand column, formed by the "Julia" Alpine Division, broke through the advanced Greek positions, then their main position, pushed up the Aóos valley and took the village of Vovoússa on November 2. Here the division found itself at the foot of the important Métzovon pass, crossed by the Lárisa–Yanina road, having covered some 25 miles of mountain terrain under an icy rain. On the following day a Greek counter-attack down from the heights forced the Italians into a retreat that was as hasty as it was disastrous.

In the centre, the 23rd "Ferrana" Infantry Division and the 131st "Centauro" Armoured Division, which had Yanina as their first objective, were held up by the Greek forward positions and completely halted by their main position, largely as a result of the action fought by the Greek 8th Division, acting as covering force.

In the coastal sector, the "Siena" Division was luckier. It took Filiates, crossed the raging River Thiamis, and reached Paramithia with the intention of encircling the Greek position at Yanina. At sea, appalling conditions forced Comando Supremo to abandon its projected amphibious operation against Corfu, while bad weather prevented the Italian Air Force from bringing its superiority to bear.

The Italians had lost all the advantage of surprise: the Italian bombers were not able to slow down the mobilisation and concentration of the Greek forces; and all the weaknesses of the plan adopted on the recommendation of Visconti-Prasca were now obvious. By November 12 General Papagos had at the front over 100 infantry battalions fighting in terrain to which they were accustomed, compared with less than 50 Italian battalions.

Visconti-Prasca was dismissed on November 9 and was replaced by General Ubaldo Soddu, Under-Secretary of State for War and Deputy Chief-of-Staff of the Army. He now found two armies under his command: on the right, General Carlo Gelosa's 11th Army, and on the left General Mario Vercellino's 9th Army. But until the remobilised divisions could be shipped across the Adriatic these units were armies only in name.

On the Greek side, General Papagos did not content himself with the success of his defensive strategy; in this war, with 45 million Italians attacking seven million Greeks, a "wait and see" policy woul&have been tantamount to an admission of defeat. Papagos determined to exploit the errors committed by the Italians and to counter-attack before the enormous numerical and material superiority of the Italian Army could be brought into play. On November 14 the Greek Army went over to the offensive along the entire front from Lake Prespa to the Ionian Sea.

On the Greek right, V Corps under General Tzolakoglou, fielding at first three and finally five divisions, broke through at Mount Morova and after eight days' fighting had destroyed the Italian 9th Army at Koritsa, taking 2,000 prisoners, 80 field guns, 55 anti-tank guns and 300 machine guns from the "Tridentina"

Mountain Division and the "Arezzo", "Parma", and "Piemonte" Infantry Divisions. This brilliant success was exploited further to the north, and on December 4 the Greek III Corps occupied Pogradec on Lake Ohrida.

On November 21 the II Corps under General Papadopoulos also crossed the Albanian frontier, despite the formidable obstacle of the Grámmos massif, and took Ersekë and Leskovik. This gave the Greek High Command an excellent front between the Koritsa plateau and the valley of the Aóos. On December 5, a gallant action gave the II Corps Përmet. 23 miles inside Albania. On the left, the I Corps under General Kosmas crossed the Thiamis on the heels of the retreating 11th Army. Pushing down the Dhrin valley, the Greek advance guards were greeted enthusiastically by the population of Argyrokastron - which says much for the deep Albanian feelings of loyalty towards Italy which Jacomoni had described to Mussolini. Two days before, the left-flank division under General Kosmas had taken Sarandë, formerly Santi Quaranta, which the Italian Fascist régime had rechristened Porto Edda.

After December 5 the Greek offensive began to peter out. The Greek Army's lack of tanks and its poverty in anti-tank weapons forced it to shun the plains and valleys in its attacks, and so the excellent Greek infantrymen concentrated on the mountain heights for their operations. But by the beginning of December temperatures in the mountains were falling as low as 15 and even 20 degrees Centigrade below zero, and these were rendered even more unbearable by severe snowstorms.

Lacking tanks, lacking even sufficient transport vehicles, the Greeks now began to experience the sufferings of their enemy. The British had no material which they could spare for their new allies. On the other hand, no less than eight Italian divisions had been shipped to Albania between October 28 and the end of December. Far too often, however, the demands of the front led General Soddu to use up his reinforcements piecemeal to plug local breakthroughs. But quite apart from this, the supply of Italian reinforcements was badly organised.

However, the comparatively rapid supply of Italian reinforcements only raised fresh problems with regard to their supplies. On December 4 the Quartermaster-General, Scuero, described the depôt and magazine supplies as almost completely exhausted.

No one could deny the victor's laurels to the Greek soldier. But under conditions like these one can only say that the Italian soldier had earned the martyr's crown a thousand times over.

Taranto

Meanwhile, the British Mediterranean Fleet had struck as deadly a blow as the Greek Army. From the moment when the aircraft-carrier Illustrious joined his command, Cunningham detected a certain lack of offensive spirit in the Italian squadron based on Taranto. This led to the preparation of a British torpedo-bombing attack, to be known as Operation "Judgement".

The first idea of Rear-Admiral Lyster, commanding the British carrier force in the Mediterranean, had been to attack on the night of October 21, the anniversary of Trafalgar; but an accident aboard Illustrious forced him to postpone "Judgement" until

November 11, when the phase of the moon would next favour the venture. Then he had to operate without the aircraft-carrier Eagle, which transferred some of her Swordfish aircraft to Illustrious, however. Despite all this, Cunningham put to sea on November 6 to cooperate with a sortie by Force H, which was escorting the battleship Barham on its journey to the eastern Mediterranean.

On the evening of November 11 an air reconnaissance from Malta carried out by Martin Marylands and Short Sunderlands established that all six of the Italian battleships were in port. Having steamed to within 190 miles of Taranto, Lyster flew off his 21 Swordfish in two waves. Eleven of them were fitted with torpedoes and the other ten with bombs and flares.

Several circumstances favoured the attackers. A few days before, a heavy storm had driven down several balloons from the barrage protecting the Taranto anchorage. The anti-torpedo nets surrounding the warships only extended 26 feet down while the British torpedoes, set to detonate either on contact or by magnetic proximity, ran at 30 feet. Finally, when the alert was sounded, the Italians did not activate the harbour smokescreens, in order not to impair the fire of the anti-aircraft guns. Nevertheless, the Fleet Air Arm crews needed all their dash and gallantry to penetrate the fire of the 21 100-mm batteries and the 200 light A.A. guns, quite apart from the guns aboard the warships, mark their targets, and drop their torpedoes accurately.

Eleven torpedoes were launched, and six scored hits: three on the Littorio, two on the Duilio, and one on the Cavour. The last Swordfish returned to Illustrious at about 0300 hours. The British lost only two aircraft. In reply, the Italian land batteries alone had

Taranto attack - Italian battleship Duilio after attack by Swordfish.

fired some 8,500 shells. Of the aircraft crews, one was killed and three others were taken prisoner. Littorio and Duilio were out of action for the next six months and needed considerable repairs. The older Cavour was raised, towed from Taranto to Trieste, and abandoned there. Until the summer of 1941 Supermarina's battle fleet was reduced to three battleships, which permitted Admiral Cunningham to release the elderly British battleships Ramillies and Malaya for much-needed escort duties on the Atlantic convoy routes.

This series of disasters caused near chaos in the Italian High Command. Refusing to put the blame Where it belonged — on his own vanity — Mussolini decided to make a scapegoat of

North Africa - an Italian bomb explodes.

Marshal Badoglio. But as the Commander-in-Chief of the Italian Armed Forces could hardly level a public indictment against his own Chief of General Staff, Mussolini opened his campaign against Badoglio with a vicious editorial aimed at the Marshal by Roberto Farinacci, editor of the official paper Regime Fascista. Badoglio demanded a public retraction of this allegation that he was not only incompetent but had also betrayed Mussolini's trust by ignorance or deliberate treachery. When he was refused all satisfaction, Badoglio resigned on November 26.

General Ugo Cavallero stepped into his place. Apart from the torrent of defamation poured on his character in Ciano's diary, it must be said that Cavallero was a much-discussed figure among his fellow generals, and that a period of involvement in the arms industry had not added to his prestige. Admiral Cavagnari was dismissed as head of Supermarina and Under-Secretary of State for the Navy and was replaced by Admiral Arturo Riccardi, a fact which publicly branded the former as the man responsible for the Taranto fiasco. Finally, de Vecchi resigned and was replaced by General Ettore Bastico as Governor of the Aegean.

Although Hitler was infuriated by the disasters which his friend and ally had brought down on himself, the interests of the Reich nevertheless made it essential for the Wehrmacht to retrieve the situation. On November 18, at the Berghof, Hitler made himself clear to Ciano: he had only sent German troops into Rumania to safeguard the Ploie ti oil wells from Soviet machinations, and now they would be within range of R.A.F. bombers if the British set up air bases in Greece. He therefore proposed to invade Greece via Bulgaria, and set the provisional date at around March 15.

But this new plan of Hitler's meant that Mussolini must reverse his entire policy towards Yugoslavia. Instead of the aggressive attitude which Mussolini had always kept up, it was now essential to bring Yugoslavia into the Axis. Ciano, however, had reservations about the political decisions which governed Hitler's military intervention in the Balkans. It was clear to him that from now on Italy would not be waging a war aimed at her own interests, and that the future relations between Mussolini and Hitler would be those of vassal and lord.

The day after Ciano's departure from Berchtesgaden, Hitler and Ribbentrop put their cards on the table before the Spanish Foreign Minister, Serrano Suñer. On November 12 Hitler had ordered the preliminary moves for Operation "Felix", which was to capture Gibraltar. It was vital to waste no further time in establishing Franco's final intentions.

Suñer restated the arguments which had been put forward at Hendaye. The capture of Gibraltar, he declared, would not pay full dividends until the Italians had taken Port Said, the key to the other entrance to the Mediterranean. Moreover, Spain would need nearly 400,000 tons of cereals and two months to prepare for war. For all his powers of persuasion, Hitler failed to get Suñer to modify this point of view. Suffer left the Berghof without having accepted anything, but — and this was probably even more important — without having issued a flat refusal.

The Italian defeats at Koritsa and Taranto had certainly done much to influence Franco's decision. In less than a month, the further defeat at Sidi Barrani would confirm the Caudillo in his policy of non-belligerence.

Battle at Sidi Barrani

The Italian forces around Sidi Barrani had severe weaknesses in their deployment. In the first line, General Gallina's Libyan Corps held the 19 miles between Maktila on the coast and Nibeiwa in the desert. In reserve, General Merzari's "3rd of January" Black Shirt Division, occupying Sidi Barrani itself, was some 12 miles back from the units which it would be required to support. In the second line, XXI Corps (General Dalmazzo) had its "Cirene" Division dug in on the escarpment, 20 miles west of Nibeiwa. The area between the two points was only weakly patrolled.

Such a strung-out disposition was fatally vulnerable to an armoured attack. As it could not be adjusted within 24 hours it exposed the Italian Army, "motorised on foot", as a wag referred to it, to piecemeal destruction. In addition, the rocky terrain had prevented an anti-tank ditch from being dug, and there were not enough mines and too few 47-mm anti-tank guns to repel an armoured advance.

Egyptian troops in a Vickers light tank.

Matters were worsened by Italian Intelligence's failure to grasp British plans. Graziani believed that the British were over 200,000 strong — a wildly exaggerated figure. But it did not prevent him giving permission for General Berti to go to Italy at the end of November. At the front, there was the impression that something was afoot, but the increase in British motorised patrols had not caused the Italians to change their dispositions before December 9.

By then it was too late. At dawn on the 9th, surging forward from their concentration-point in the desert (which had been christened "Piccadilly Circus") the British 7th Armoured Division and 4th Indian Division struck through the gap in the Italian front, while a brigade under Brigadier A. R. Selby attacked Maktila on the coast road. The entire force, soon to be known as XIII Corps, was under the command of Lieutenant-General Richard O'Connor, and consisted of only 36,000 men and 225 armoured vehicles; among the latter were 57 Infantry tanks known as "Matildas", whose massive armour was proof against the Italian shells.

The 4th Indian Division and the Matilda tank battalion attacked Nibeiwa, which was defended by the Maletti Motorised Group. Surprise was complete, for the uproar of the artillery and air bombardment drowned the noise of engines and tank tracks, and the British were attacking from the south-west and even from the west. Badly wounded, General Maletti fought on until he was killed at the head of his troops, but by 0830 it was all over. For the price of 56 dead, Major-General Beresford-Peirse, commanding 4th Indian Division, had taken 2,000 prisoners.

Encamped at Tummar, General Pescatori of the 2nd Libyan Division planned to march to the sound of the guns as soon as the British attack began. But 4th Indian Division and the Matildas saved him the trouble. Thrown back, Pescatori counterattacked with spirit, but his forces were broken up by crushing British artillery fire. Tummar West fell in the afternoon while Tummar East did not surrender until dawn on the 10th.

In the evening of December 9, Brigadier J. A. L. Caunter's 7th Armoured Division reached the sea, cutting off the retreat of the survivors of the 2nd Libyan Division. Facing Sidi Barrani, Selby Force had thrown General Sibille's 1st Libyan Division (not without some trouble) out of its position at Maktila. The Italian pocket thus formed at Maktila was cleaned up with the assistance of British naval bombardment, a task which had been completed by the evening of the 11th.

During the same day Graziani ordered XXI Corps to fall back immediately to the Halfaya–Sollum–Capuzzo line on the frontier. The "Cirene" Division got the order in time and fell back without trouble. But this was not the case with General Spinelli's "Catanzaro" Division, thanks to an error in transmission. It was caught on the move between Buqbuq and Sollum and half annihilated.

This last defeat raised the losses of the Italian 10th Army to 38,000 prisoners, 237 guns, and 73 tanks, while the British losses amounted to only 624 killed, wounded, and missing. But O'Connor's force had no sooner won this glorious and virtually painless victory than it was seriously weakened by the withdrawal of the excellent 4th Indian Division, which was earmarked for the campaign against the Italians in Eritrea.

It is now clear that this was a mistake. In Italian East Africa the Duke of Aosta, Viceroy of Abyssinia, was already so weak that the Anglo-Egyptian Sudan had nothing to fear from his forces, and the same applied to Kenya. The 4th Indian Division was badly missed in the Western Desert.

Was Wavell to blame? Certainly, the original scope of Operation "Compass", the attack on the Italians at Sidi Barrani, was limited to a five-day raid after which O'Connor was to fall back on Marsa Matrûh. But the real responsibility lay much higher. The British War Cabinet was deeply concerned with Abyssinia, and Churchill was at the same time trying to interest the Imperial General Staff in a venture called Operation "Workshop", directed against the Italian island of Pantelleria in the Mediterranean.

The 6th Australian Division (Major-General I. G. Mackay) replaced 4th Indian Division in XIII Corps. But General O'Connor did not wait for its arrival before launching an all-out pursuit against the beaten and disorganised Italian forces. On December 14 he crossed the frontier south of Capuzzo, swung his armoured and motorised forces to the north, and invaded Bardia on the 18th. The Bardia perimeter, 24 miles in extent, was defended by General Bergonzoli's XXIII Corps, with the survivors of the "Catanzaro" and "Cirene" Divisions from Egypt, General Tracchia's "Marmarica" Division, and General Antonelli's "23rd of March" Black Shirt Division — a total force of 45,000 men and 430 guns.

On December 18, General Mackay's 6th Australian Division joined XIII Corps. Prospects for the Axis darkened with the fall of Bardia right at the beginning of 1941; not even the first major fire raid on London on the night of December 30–31 did much to redress the balance. In the occupied or threatened countries of Europe there was a widespread feeling that the defeat of Mussolini would only be a matter of time, and that that of Hitler would follow.

But in view of the military weakness of Great Britain and her Empire, this was very far from the truth …

Opening shots of the battle of Tripoli.

After receiving this reassuring confirmation of Greece's intentions, the British Government made no attempt to influence the Greek Government. On January 21, the very day of the attack on Tobruk, London, now free from any urgent Greek commitments, ordered G.H.Q. Cairo to resume its offensive towards Benghazi without further delay.

After the surprise attack on Sidi Barrani, Marshal Graziani had given his opinion that Cyrenaica could no longer be defended and that it would be advisable to withdraw to Tripoli, putting the Sirte Desert between his 10th Army and the Army of the Nile. When the Italian High Command recommended him to be more optimistic, Graziani set to work to improvise the defence of

Cyrenaica-but it must be admitted that he did not make a very good job of it. His 10th Army was divided into three defensive groups: XXIII Corps at Bardia, XXII Corps at Tobruk, and the XX Corps (General Cona) holding the Mechili-Derna line. This disposition meant that it was highly likely that 10th Army could be defeated piece meal by an enemy who was greatly inferior in overall numbers.

On January 9, despite the destruction of XXIII Corps in the battle for Bardia, Graziani was now showing optimism instead of his previous pessimism. In fact the Jebel Akhdar, the massif between Mechili and Derna which rises to a height of about 1,650 feet, was quite unsuitable for an attack by mechanised forces.

By putting an infantry division into the Derna position and

the armoured brigade of General Babini into Mechili, Graziani thought he would have an excellent chance of halting the British advance towards Benghazi. But he was forgetting that those two formations would have to fight independently as they were separated by the Jebel Akhdar hills and could not reinforce one another.

On January 24 the 6th Australian Division approached the Derna position, while the 7th Armoured Division fell upon Babini's armoured brigade, in spite of the extremely poor state of the British tanks. The Italian 14-ton tanks were fighting the same number of 12.5-ton British cruiser tanks, and the battle ended badly for the Italians. They retreated into the Jebel Akhdar to avoid encirclement — but in so doing they gave the British a clear road to the main Italian supply-line along the Gulf of Sirte. For this reason Graziani decided to abandon western Cyrenaica on February 1. General Gariboldi was sent to Tripoli to organise the defence of the province, and General Tellera succeeded him as commander of 10th Army.

The distance between Mechili and Beda Fomm, near the Gulf of Sirte, is about 140 miles. Along the coast road between Derna and Beda Fomm the distance is about 225 miles. But the retreating Italians had the advantage of using the Via Balbia, the excellent coast road; the British, advancing from Mechili towards Beda Fomm, had only a poorly reconnoitred track, which was not clearly marked and which crossed a desert consisting either of soft sand or of areas strewn with large rocks.

"War is won with leftovers", Marshal Foch had once said. It is hardly likely that Generals O'Connor and O'Moore Creagh,

commander of 7th Armoured Division, had ever heard of this dictum, but now they put it into practice with a vengeance. At 1500 hours on February 4 the 11th Hussars (Colonel Combe) were at Msus, only 60 miles from the Via Balbia. At dawn on the 5th, after they had been reinforced with some artillery, they took the track leading to Antelat and at noon reached their objective at Beda Fomm, half an hour before the first Italian column retreating from Benghazi down the Via Balbia. Confused engagements were fought throughout February 6, with the Italians hitting out wildly as they came up against the British blocking their retreat.

Finally, at 0900 hours on February 7, O'Connor sent an uncoded signal for the information of Wavell and the edification of Mussolini: "Fox killed in the open." Badly wounded, General Tellera died a few hours later; the H.Q. of 10th Army, and Generals Cona and Babini, had been captured. General Bergonzoli had also been captured: he had managed to make his way through the Australian lines when Bardia fell. About 20,000 Italians were also captured, and the final count of the equipment seized by the British after this last battle amounted to 112 11- and 14-ton M11 and M13 medium tanks, 216 guns, and 1,500 vehicles.

On February 3 the British had reached El Agheila at the bottom of the Gulf of Sirte. This was a very important position, for there was only a narrow gap about 15–20 miles wide through which tanks could pass between the desert and the sea. As the British XIII Corps now commanded this position, it was well placed to invade Tripolitania or defend Cyrenaica as required.

Wavell's original five-day raid had developed into a two-month campaign. In four pitched battles O'Connor had advanced 560 miles from his starting position. Although he never had more than two divisions under his command, he had destroyed one Italian army (four corps, or nine divisions) at a cost of only 500 dead, 1,373 wounded, and 56 missing. The "bag" of Italian prisoners amounted to 130,000 men, including 22 generals and one admiral, and O'Connor had seized or destroyed 845 guns and 380 tanks. For the third time in the war Guderian's words to Hitler had been proved true: "Tanks are a life-saving weapon".

Admiral Sir Andrew Cunningham was born in 1883. In 1939 he was C.-in-C., Mediterranean, and when Italy entered the war he soon found himself outnumbered and in difficult straits strategically and logistically. He quickly wrested command from the Italians, however, in several actions at sea and at Taranto, and thus secured the army's right flank. Cunningham became Allied Naval C.-in-C. under Eisenhower in 1943, and First Sea Lord in October of the same year.

The Luftwaffe strikes

On December 27, after the battle of Sidi Barrani, Graziani had attempted to explain matters to Mussolini. "From the harsh experience of these bitter days," he wrote, "we must conclude that in this theatre of war a single armoured division is more powerful than a whole army."

Coming events would prove these to be prophetic words.

The Wehrmacht's intervention in the Mediterranean theatre began when the German High Command transferred X Fliegerkorps to Sicily and Calabria.

At the end of December 1940, General Geissler of the Luftwaffe set up his H.Q. at Taormina. His squadrons were divided between the airfields at Catania, Comiso, Marsala, Trdpani, Palermo, and Reggio di Calabria, along with 45 Italian bombers and 75 Italian fighters. Together with the 70 bombers and 25 fighters of the Regia Aeronautica based in Sardinia, the number of Axis aircraft capable of operating in the central Mediterranean, which narrows to under 90 miles between Cape Bon in Tunisia and Marsala in Sicily, was approximately 400.

Such a force should normally have been under the command of Superaero, the High Command of the Italian Air Force. But Göring had no intention of permitting this, for he deliberately kept "his" airmen under his own control and reserved to himself the right to give them orders. Thus it is fairly certain that he was responsible for continual interference and fraction in the conduct of operations.

The strength of the R.A.F. on Malta was far smaller. When X Fliegerkorps moved south, the British air defences of Malta consisted of a dozen Swordfish, 16 Hurricanes, 16 Wellington twin-engine bombers, and a few Martin Maryland bomber/reconnaissance aircraft built in the United States. Admittedly a new shipload of 16 Hurricanes was expected with the next convoy from Gibraltar, but this was still a drop in the ocean.

General Geissler and his aircrews got their first chance to distinguish themselves with the British Operation "Excess", which started on January 6. Admiral Somerville's task was to convoy four merchantmen (one for Malta, the others for Greece) from Gibraltar to the central Mediterranean. Admiral Cunningham in

Night photo of enemy air attack on new British forward positions.

Alexandria would make use of the appearance of Force H in the Western Mediterranean to send two merchantment into Malta. At the same time, two cruisers from his light forces would take troops there. After that he would take charge of the ships making for Greece from Gibraltar.

While the two British convoys converged on Malta from east and west, the Malta-based bombers struck at Naples on the night of January 8–9. Their target was the Italian battleships which had survived the Taranto raid. The Giulio Cesare suffered a leak as the result of a bomb explosion on the bottom of the harbour and had to steam to Genoa for repairs. The Vittorio Veneto escaped untouched, but Supermarina decided to transfer her to La Spezia,

where she would be out of range of the Malta-based bombers. This, however, would prevent Vittorio Veneto from taking any useful action in the narrows between Tunisia and Sicily.

Force H completed its mission without incident. Somerville passed to the south of Sardinia on the evening of January 9 and returned to Gibraltar with the battleship Malaya, the battle-cruiser Renown, and the aircraft-carrier Ark Royal, leaving his charges under the protection of an A.A. cruiser, two heavy cruisers (Gloucester and Southampton, which had joined him after landing the troops they had brought from Alexandria in Malta), and five destroyers. At dawn on January 10 the Gloucester and Southampton sank the Italian torpedo-boat Vega which had tried heroically to attack them. During this action, the destroyer

Australian soldiers with gramaphone at entrance to bunker.

Gallant hit a mine and had to be towed to Malta. Repairs proved impossible, however, because of Axis air attacks.

Help for Mussolini

The Italian defeats in Albania, at Taranto and in Libya were a cause of deep concern for the Germans. The Luftwaffe's X Fliegerkorps was sent to bases in Sicily at the end of December 1940 to close the Mediterranean to the British between Sicily and Tunisia and to fight British aircraft based on Malta.

On January 3, 1941, Australian forces took Bardia in Libya. On January 21 the British captured Tobruk. Having made these important inroads into Mussolini's North American Empire, the British now turned their attention to the support of Greece. It was estimated that the Germans had at least 12 divisions in Rumania and the Greek General Papagos believed that the Greeks would need to be reinforced with nine British divisions. The British offer was more modest, amounting to little more than two or three divisions along with an air formation.

Ordeal of the Illustrious

But Cunningham's Mediterranean Fleet did not get off so easily. Towards 1230 hours Junkers Ju 87 and Ju 88 bombers appeared over the British fleet, which had joined the convoy soon after the sinking of the Vega. They launched a fierce attack on the aircraft-carrier Illustrious, in spite of sustained fire from the battleships Warspite and Valiant.

"There was no doubt we were watching complete experts," wrote Admiral Cunningham in his memoirs. "Formed roughly in a larger circle over the fleet they peeled off one by one when reaching the attacking position. We could not but admire the skill and precision of it all. The attacks were pressed home to point-blank range, and as they pulled out of their dives some of them were seen to fly along the flight deck of the Illustrious below the level of her funnel."

Illustrious was struck by two 550-lb and four 1,100-lb bombs in under 10 minutes, and but for her armoured flight deck she would most likely have suffered the same fate as many American and British aircraft-carriers in the Far East. Nevertheless she was badly damaged; her steering-gear was out of action and she had to steer with her propellers. Admiral Cunningham therefore ordered her to return to Malta for repairs.

On its return voyage the following day Cunningham's force was again attacked by the dive-bombers of X Fliegerkorps. The luckless Southampton was disabled and set on fire; she had to be abandoned by her crew and was sunk by torpedoes.

At Malta, workers and engineers laboured frantically to get Illustrious ready for action again. But on January 16 she received more damage from German bombs, which was patched up, after a fashion. On the night of January 23 Illustrious left the Grand Harbour and returned to Alexandria, making the remarkable speed of 28 knots. Nevertheless, she had to be completely overhauled and set out on a long voyage to the American yards at Norfolk, Virginia, which undertook the work with the sympathetic agreement of President Roosevelt.

In the absence of Illustrious the Admiralty decided that the carrier Formidable, which was in the Atlantic, should proceed to Alexandria round the Cape of Good Hope. Without fleet air cover, Admiral Cunningham was unable to take any action in the waters south of Sicily until Formidable joined his flag, which she did, in spite of the Luftwaffe's attempts to mine the Suez Canal and the approaches to Alexandria, on March 10.

Meanwhile the German bombers based in Sicily kept Malta under constant air bombardment. Heavy losses were inflicted on the island's aircraft, which were under the command of Air Vice-Marshal H. P. Lloyd. At the end of February the surviving Wellington bombers had to be brought back to Egypt; the fighters had been suffering similar losses, and on March 11 the Hurricanes, the only aircraft on Malta capable of tackling the Messerschmitt 109's and 110's on anything like equal terms, were reduced to eight battleworthy machines.

From March 1941, however, the need for air support for the Afrika Korps and for Operation "Marita" in the Balkans compelled General Geissler to divert a large number of his squadrons to these new operational theatres. The inevitable result was a slackening of the pressure put on Malta by X Fliegerkorps. Between April 3 and May 21 Force H was able to supply Malta with 82 Hurricanes, flown from the carriers Ark Royal and Furious.

Field Marshall Erwin Rommel.

For 18 months, between March 1941 and September 1942, Erwin Rommel displayed outstanding ability to attack and to manoeuvre, learning to combine cunning with force. There is no doubt that the man who managed to rebound from a decisive defeat before Tobruk into an advance which took him to the gates of Alexandria must be counted among the truly great commanders of all time.

But was his brilliance as a tactician matched by his strategic ability? This is not so clear. One firm criterion of sound strategy is that it must combine the different interests of land, sea, and air forces into a framework which Churchill described with the ugly word "triphibian". And Rommel repeatedly failed to do this.

During the summer of 1942, for example, Rommel constantly blamed Comando Supremo for the frequent breakdowns in his supply system, forgetting that after taking Tobruk on June 21 he had assured Cavallero that he would be able to reach the Nile with the help of the fuel and transport captured in Tobruk. He also forgot that although he was keeping Luftwaffe squadrons from the task of neutralising Malta, the British bombers, torpedo-bombers, and submarines based on the island were exacting a merciless toll on the Italian merchant tonnage in the central Mediterranean. In fact, it was on Rommel's urgent request — despite the protests of Kesselring and Cavallero — that Hitler and Mussolini gave up Operation "Hercules", which could and should have presented the Axis with Malta and Gozo.

Whatever one may think of Rommel in a historical context, his former subordinates and opponents all pay tribute to his nobility of character and his high moral code. Undoubtedly his task in fighting a "clean war" in the African desert was easier than that of his colleagues on the Eastern Front, who had the partisans and Hitler to deal with. But when slight scuffles broke out between his troops and Arab tribesmen, whom British agents were trying to enlist against the Italians, Rommel noted in his diary on September 16, 1942: "There is nothing so unpleasant as partisan warfare. It is perhaps very important not to make reprisals on hostages at the first outbreak of partisan warfare, for these only create feelings of revenge and serve to strengthen the franc-tireurs. It is better to allow an incident to go unavenged than to hit back at the innocent. It only agitates the whole neighbourhood, and hostages easily become martyrs."

In 1944 Rommel protested to Hitler in the same spirit of humanity, good sense, and true German patriotism against the appalling massacre of French civilians at Oradour-sur-Glane perpetrated by the S.S. Das Reich Panzer Division, and demanded exemplary punishment for those responsible for the crime. (The result was a coarse and violent rebuff.) The honourable treatment which Rommel offered to the Free French prisoners taken at Bir Hakeim in June 1942 should also be noted. It ignored the fact that the Franco-German armistice of 1940, according to the rules and usages of war, had deprived de Gaulle's Free French adherents of the status and privileges of regular combatants.

Rommel was also an attentive husband, who wrote to his wife every day to keep her in touch with his fortunes. The following extracts come from two successive letters (the second contains a thinly-veiled reference to his new assignment in Africa).

"February 6, 1941

"Dearest Lu,

"Landed at Staaken 12.45. First to C.in-C. Army, who appointed me to my new job, and then to Führer. Things are moving fast. My kit is coming on here. I can only take barest necessities with me. Perhaps I'll be able to get the rest out soon. I need not tell you that my head is swimming with all the many things there are to be done. It'll be months before anything materialises.

"So 'our leave' was cut short again. Don't be sad, it had to be. The new job is very big and important."

"February 7, 1941.

"Slept on my new job last night. It's one way of getting my rheumatism treatment. I've got a lot to do, in the few hours that remain, getting together all I need."

This was typical of Rommel. And one can only conclude that when his widow and his son, Manfred, chose the title War Without Hate for the collection of letters and memoirs which he left, it was a perfectly appropriate decision.

The British and the Greeks

While the advance units of the Afrika Korps were leaving Italy for Africa General Wavell in Cairo was carrying out the orders he had received from London. The 6th Australian Division, the 2nd New Zealand Division (Major-General B. C. Freyberg) and over half the 2nd Armoured Division (Major-General M. D. Gambier-

Parry), which had just arrived from England, were to be sent to help the Greeks.

Brigadier E. Dorman-Smith, an officer of G.H.Q. Middle East in Cairo, who had been at the front with O'Connor from Mechili to Beda Fomm, returned to Cairo to see Wavell at 1000 hours on February 12 (a few hours, in fact, before Rommel called on Gariboldi in Tripoli), and heard about this new change of front from Wavell, Dorman-Smith remarked that while he had been away from G.H.Q. the usual maps of the Western Desert on the walls had been replaced by maps of Greece, and that Wavell commented sardonically: "You see, Eric, I'm starting my spring campaign."

On the previous day Wavell had in fact cabled Churchill after receiving a message from Lieutenant-General Sir Henry Maitland Wilson in Tobruk, informing him that the Italian forces were in a state of collapse. At the front, O'Connor stated that he was ready to move forward into Tripolitania if all available troops were sent to reinforce his 7th Armoured Division, and if the R.A.F. and Admiral Cunningham's Inshore Squadron (one monitor and three gunboats) could harass the Italian-held coastline and give him the necessary support. On the latter assumption he had planned amphibious operations against Buerat and subsequently against Misurata, further along the coast.

O'Connor's optimism was matched in Tripoli by Rommel's initial pessimism. The latter had just received a discouraging report from Lieutenant Heggenreiner, a German liaison officer in North Africa. Rommel noted that Heggenreiner" described some very unpleasant incidents which had occurred during the retreat, or rather the rout which it had become. Italian troops had thrown away their weapons and ammunition and clambered on to overloaded vehicles in a wild attempt to get away to the west. This had led to some ugly scenes, and even to shooting. Morale was as low as it could be in all military circles in Tripoli. Most of the Italian officers had already packed their bags and were hoping for a quick return trip to Italy."

General Gariboldi now had only five divisions under his orders: the "Bologna", "Brescia", "Pavia", "Sabratha", and "Savona" Divisions. Even on June 10, 1940, these were considered "inefficient", and had since had orders to give up part of their equipment to the recently-destroyed 10th Army. But for the formal orders of the British War Cabinet, nothing could have kept O'Connor and the victors of Sidi Barrani, Bardia, Tobruk, Mechili, and Beda Fomm from driving through to Tripoli.

But Churchill had already made his decision, and it was adhered to. For once Sir John Dill, the C.I.G.S., supported the Prime Minister's view. But Brooke, still C.-in-C., Home Forces, believed that Churchill's decision overreached the possibilities of British strategy, considering the means then available. Brooke later wrote: "This is one of the very few occasions on which I doubted Dill's advice and judgement, and I am not in a position to form any definite opinion as I was not familiar with all the facts. I have, however, always considered from the very start that our participation in the operations in Greece was a definite strategic blunder. Our hands were more than full at that time in the Middle East, and Greece could only result in the most dangerous dispersal of force."

Brooke's fears were certainly proved correct by the course of events. But the British felt themselves bound to go to the aid of the Greeks, quite apart from the fact that a refusal to do so would have been a gift for the Axis propagandists. There was always the possibility that without British help the Greeks might have been tempted to negotiate some arrangement with Hitler. On the other hand, the sending of a British expeditionary force to Greece proved to the world that Britain was not pursuing a policy of national self-interest. Despite the defeats in Greece and Crete, the attempt did much to save British prestige — more so than if it had not been made. The same cannot be said for projects such as Operation "Mandible", which compelled Wavell to keep the 7th Australian Division in the Nile Delta for a possible attack on Rhodes and Leros.

The desert front

As G.H.Q. Cairo was forced to give up the troops for this expeditionary force, it was left with only skeleton forces to "consolidate" its position in western Cyrenaica, according to orders. These forces consisted mainly of the rump of the 2nd Armoured Division, which had been equipped with captured Italian vehicles to replace the tanks sent to Greece. But the Italian tanks were so poor that even good British crews could not improve their performance. The 9th Australian Division (Major-General L. J. Morshead) should have reinforced this so-called armoured formation, but because of supply difficulties its foremost units had not got beyond Tobruk. The 3rd Indian Motorised Brigade completed this mediocre force.

Australian troops under heavy fire in Libya.

After the capture of Benghazi, Wavell had appointed General Maitland Wilson as military governor of Cyrenaica. But the latter was recalled to Cairo and put in charge of the Greek expeditionary force immediately after taking up his command. He was succeeded by Lieutenant-General Philip Neame, V.C., a newcomer to the desert theatre, who only had a few days to accustom himself to the terrain.

The 7th Armoured Division, which had been the spearhead of XIII Corps, had been brought back to the Delta by Wavell to be completely refitted. Churchill had protested violently against this decision, and it is clear that if the division's repair shops could have been set up in Tobruk after its fall, Rommel's task

Rommel's staff during tour pass in German tanks.

force. Again, on March 19 Hitler, decorating Rommel with the Oak Leaves to the Knight's Cross, gave him no other instructions. According to his diaries this left Rommel, eager for action, "not very happy". Benghazi, the objective given him for his spring campaign, appeared to him to be indefensible by itself. The whole of Cyrenaica must therefore be recovered to ensure its security.

Rommel strikes

At dawn on March 24 the reconnaissance group of Rommel's 5th Light Division attacked El Agheila in Libya, and the British units defending this key position pulled back. They took up new positions at Marsa Brega, between the Gulf of Sirte and salt marsh impassable to tanks, about 50 miles south-west of Agedabia.

Rommel felt that he could not stick to the letter of his orders and so leave the British with enough time to reorganise while he waited for the whole of the 15th Panzer Division to reach the front. If he attacked again without delay he had a chance of surprising the British with his small mobile forces and of dislodging them from what was an extremely strong defensive position.

He therefore attacked again on March 31. The British did put up some resistance at Marsa Brega, but, outflanked on the desert front, they were forced to give up the place to the 5th Light Division. By the evening of April 2 the German forces, followed by the "Ariete" Armoured Division and the "Brescia" Infantry Division, occupied the Agedabia region two months ahead of the schedule set by O.K.H. About 800 British prisoners were taken during this engagement. Rommel's cunning use of dummy

would have been much harder. But it must be remembered that this first British desert offensive had been the result of successive improvisations. On December 9, 1940, O'Connor had set out on a five-day raid. By February 6, 1941, he was over 500 miles further west, at El Agheila. It was not surprising that in these totally unexpected circumstances the base facilities had not kept up with the advance of the tanks.

In any event the dispositions made by Wavell show clearly that he believed that any large-scale counter-offensive by Rommel was highly improbable. Brauchitsch and Halder also believed that Rommel's attack on Agedabia could not take place until the end of May, after the last units of 15th Panzer Division had joined his tanks had added to the confusion of the British as they retreated; German reconnaissance aircraft saw disorganised columns streaming back towards Benghazi and Mechili.

Rommel has often been criticised for acting incorrectly; but any subordinate is entitled to pursue his own objectives if he discovers that the ones he has been given by his superiors have been based on an incorrect appreciation of the situation. And this was precisely the position when Rommel and the Afrika Korps reached Marsa Brega at the end of March 1941.

But in such a situation a subordinate is also supposed to inform his superiors without a moment's delay of the steps he feels himself obliged to take. Rommel failed to do so, and for days he played hide and seek with his Italian and German superiors while he breathlessly exploited his initial success.

In his book on the war in Africa General Pietro Maravigna makes this quite clear. "The covering enemy troops were surprised by the attack and withdrew. They abandoned Bir es-Suera and Marsa Brega, which Rommel's advanced forces occupied on April 1, while the main body of the 5th Light Division took up its position to the east of El Agheila.

"In Tripoli, and even more so in Rome, this news came like thunder in a clear sky. Mussolini, who was very much put out, asked Rintelen for information. Rintelen had none to give. He then asked Gariboldi to explain matters. Gariboldi replied that Rommel had evaded all authority and was acting entirely on his own initiative. Moreover, Gariboldi disclaimed all responsibility, as he had only authorised Rommel to make a surprise attack on the British forces west of Marsa Brega to improve our own

defences; the German general, carried away by his initial success, had exceeded his authority."

Gariboldi subsequently set off after Rommel with the intention of stopping him, but he was very abruptly received by his impetuous subordinate, especially as fresh successes had provided further justification for his actions; and the German High Command in Berlin signalled its approval. In fact, on the night of April 3–4 the reconnaissance group of the 5th Light Division entered Benghazi, and its main body drove onwards towards Mechili.

In Cairo the news of Rommel's escapade caused as much bewilderment as it had to Comando Supremo. Neame had been ordered not to let his position be endangered if the Axis forces attacked but to make a fighting retreat; but Wavell quickly realised that Neame had been overtaken by the sudden speed of events, and that the organised retreat he had had in mind was turning into a rout.

Decision to hold Tobruk

The decision to defend Tobruk at all costs was taken by Wavell on the advice of Air Chief-Marshal Longmore and Admiral Cunningham. The garrison consisted of the 9th Australian Division, reinforced by a brigade of the 7th, an armoured regiment with 45 armoured cars, and an A.A. brigade with 16 heavy and 59 light guns. All in all, there were about 36,000 men within the Tobruk perimeter.

The assault on January 21, in which Major-General Mackay had captured Tobruk, had been so rapid that the fortifications

Rommel in conference with Italian general.

had fallen into the hands of the British almost untouched. The strongpoints, which were laid out in alternating rows, were protected by 3-foot thick concrete slabs which were proof against the heaviest guns (15-cm) the Afrika Korps had at this time. The antitank ditch was also intact and was still completely camouflaged with sandcovered planks.

But above all — if it is true that an army is as good as its commander — the strongest part of the Tobruk defences was Major-General Leslie Morshead, commander of 9th Australian Division. "There'll be no Dunkirk here!" he told his men. "If we should have to get out, we shall have to fight our way out. No surrender and no retreat."

Morshead, who had fought in World War I, had risen to the command of an infantry battalion at 28. For his bravery under fire he had been awarded the C.M.G., the D.S.O., and the Légion d'Honneur, and had been six times mentioned in despatches. His soldiers called him "Ming the Merciless" because of his iron discipline. Another factor favouring the defenders was the comparative narrowness of the battlefield, which prevented Rommel from making his customary surprise manoeuvres.

General (later Field-Marshal) Erwin Rommel was born in Heidenheim in 1891. He served with distinction in World War I. In 1938 Rommel was selected to command Hitler's escort battalion in Czechoslovakia and later in Poland, and he was appointed to the command of 7th Panzer Division in

February 1940. Rommel led 7th Panzer with such success during the campaign in France that it became known as the "Ghost Division", confirming Hitler's confidence in Rommel as a daring and resourceful commander.

Rommel halted at Tobruk

On April 10 Rommel tried to storm Tobruk by launching a motorised detachment under General von Prittwitz, commander of the 15th Panzer Division, to cut the coast road. But the detachment was repulsed by heavy gunfire and its commander was killed by a shell. During the night of April 13–14, a battalion of the 5th Light Division succeeded in finding a way through the minefields and crossing the anti-tank ditch. Rommel stated, however, that:

"The division's command had not mastered the art of concentrating its strength at one point, forcing a breakthrough, rolling up and securing the flanks on either side, and then penetrating like lightning, before the enemy had time to react, deep into his rear." For this reason the Panzer regiment of the 5th Light Division was overwhelmed by the concentrated fire of the Australian artillery and was unable to support the battalion which had made a "fingerprobe" advance into the defences. The latter battalion was counter-attacked and virtually destroyed, leaving 250 prisoners in the hands of the Australians. Rommel was incensed by this failure, which he punished by sacking General Streich.

The Italian divisions (the "Brescia" Infantry Division, "Trento" Motorised Division, and "Ariete" Armoured Division) were even less fortunate. On the other hand, the Afrika Korps units covering the rear of the troops attacking Tobruk reoccupied the former Axis frontier positions at Sollum, Halfaya, and Capuzzo and now stood on the Egyptian frontier. But they were considerably dispersed, and although 15th Panzer Division had now joined him, Rommel realised at last that he would only be able to capture Tobruk with a well-organised attack. He lacked the resources to do this, and the regrets he expressed to O.K.H. met with a chilly reception on the part of Brauchitsch and Halder.

Rommel is called to heel

Halder's note dated April 23 shows this clearly. "I have a feeling that things are in a mess. He [Rommel] spends his time rushing about between his widely-scattered units and sending out reconnaissance raids in which he fritters away his strength … no one knows exactly how his troops are deployed, nor the strength of their fighting capacity … He has had heavy losses as a result of piecemeal attacks. In addition his vehicles are in a bad state because of the wear and tear caused by the desert sand and many of the tank engines need replacing. Our air transport can't meet Rommel's crazy demands; we haven't enough petrol anyway, and the planes sent to North Africa wouldn't have enough fuel for the return flight."

But whatever Halder thought, he could only express it in his private diary, as Hitler retained full confidence in Rommel. In these circumstances, and with the approval of Brauchitsch, he merely sent Lieutenant-General Paulus, the Quartermaster-General of O.K.H., out to the North African front to obtain first-hand information.

Paulus, Halder thought, because of his old friendship for Rommel, would "perhaps be capable of exerting some influence to head off this soldier who has gone stark mad". The special envoy of the German Army High Command carried out his delicate mission satisfactorily-but a few weeks later the entire North African theatre was transferred from O.K.H. to O.K.W. This change of the command structure eliminated any further causes of friction between the impulsive Rommel and the methodical Halder. Halder has been criticised for being unduly cautious, because his fears did not materialise. But he had no way of knowing how small were the reserve forces at the disposal of the British C.-in-C. Halder was relying on the information of his Intelligence experts, who estimated that Wavell had 21 divisions, six of which were actually fighting or in the area between Tobruk, Sollum, and Halfaya.

As already mentioned, the Axis convoys which carried the 5th Light Division to North Africa had suffered insignificant losses. But the ships which carried 15th Panzer Division had a harder time.

Malta Submarines

During the first period of Luftwaffe ascendancy over Malta the main attack force based on the island consisted of the submarine flotilla, which made constant patrols against the Axis supply-lines to Tripoli. The odds were stacked heavily against the British submarines, and between April-August 1941 five of them were sunk. But between January and May of that year they accounted

for 16 out of the 31 Axis ships sunk while carrying supplies and reinforcements to North Africa-a striking achievement. Simultaneous patrols were made by the destroyer flotillas based on Gibraltar and Alexandria.

From the time of his first meeting with General Geissler of X Fliegerkorps, Rommel had asked that the efforts of the German bombers should be concentrated against the port of Benghazi. Later, X Fltegerkorps had given very efficient air cover to the advance of the Afrika Korps between Agedabia and Tobruk, making up to a large extent for the heavy artillery which Rommel lacked.

The inevitable result of this was that the former pressure being applied to Malta by these air forces became considerably lighter. Admiral Cunningham was not slow to exploit this welcome and unexpected respite. Early in April he transferred a flotilla of the most modern destroyers from Alexandria to Valletta. This small force, commanded by Captain P. J. Mack, scored its first success on the night of April 14–15. It surprised an Axis convoy of five merchantmen escorted by three destroyers about 35 miles off Sfax. The convoy was silhouetted against the moon while Mack's ships were in darkness. Surprise was complete. The merchantmen were reduced to wrecks within a few minutes; 350 men, 300 vehicles, and 3,500 tons of equipment for the Afrika Korps were lost. The Italian destroyer Baleno was sunk, but Captain de Cristoforo of the Tartgo, with a leg shot off by a British shell, managed to launch three torpedoes before sinking with his ship. Two of these torpedoes hit and sank the British destroyer Mohawk.

The third Italian escort destroyer, the Lampo, was totally

disabled and stranded on the shoals of the Kerkenna Bank, together with the German merchantman Arta. Lampo was recovered by the Italians in August and subsequently recommissioned — but in the meantime a group of French Resistance men from Tunisia had searched the derelicts by night, seized the ships' papers, and had passed on all information about the Afrika Korps' order of battle to Malta.

The work of the British destroyers was supplemented by that of the British submarines based on Malta and Alexandria. On February 25 the Upright (Lieutenant E. D. Norman) had scored a direct hit on the Italian light cruiser Armando

Diaz, which sank in four minutes with three-quarters of her crew. In a space of four months the British submarines in the Mediterranean sank at least a dozen Axis merchantmen, tankers, and transports between Messina and Tripoli.

The submarine Upholder, commanded by Lieutenant-Commander Malcolm Wanklyn, a brilliant submariner, particularly distinguished herself in these actions, on which the outcome of the Desert War so much depended. On the evening of May 25 Upholder sank the large Italian liner Conte Rosso (17,879 tons), and only 1,520 out of the 2,732 sailors and soldiers aboard were saved. In recognition of this Wanklyn received the Victoria Cross.

Lieutenant-Commander Malcolm David Wanklyn (second from left) and fellow submarine officers. Wanklyn rapidly emerged as the most prominent British submarine ace in the Mediterranean. The Upholder sailed on her first patrol against the Axis supply-lines to North Africa in January 1941, and Wanklyn

British artillery fire on enemy positions.

scored his first success by sinking the German transport Duisburg in the early morning of January 28. His greatest success in 1941 was the sinking of the large Italian liner Conte Rosso on May 25, for which he was awarded the Victoria Cross. In the desperate course of the Mediterranean War there was little respite for the submarine crews. Wanklyn and his crew were eventually lost when Upholder was depth-charged on April 14, 1942. He was on his twenty-third patrol and had sunk two submarines, two destroyers, and 94,900 tons of merchant shipping.

A Greek officer assists at the disembarkation of RAF personnel at the port of Athens.

On December 29, 1940, General Ugo Cavallero, the new Chief-of-Staff of the Comando Supremo, was sent over by Mussolini to relieve General Ubaldo Soddu of his command and to take control of the Italian armed forces in Albania. The Duce defined Cavallero's task in a letter dated January 1: his forces were to move over to the offensive and prove, by their energy and resolve, that doubts abroad about Italian military prestige were baseless. "Germany," the letter went on, "is ready to send a mountain division into Albania and at the same time is preparing an army to attack Greece through Bulgaria in March. I am expecting, nay, I am certain, that your intervention and the bravery of your men will show that any direct support by Germany on the Albanian front will prove to be unnecessary. The Italian nation is impatiently waiting for the wind to change."

After the war General Halder drew attention to the vexing question of German reinforcements in Albania, on which Hitler and his generals never agreed:

"When the Italians got into trouble in Albania, Hitler was inclined to send help. The Army Commander-in-Chief managed to stop the plan from being put into action, as it would have been fruitless. It was a different matter when the German forces, which were actually intended for an attack on the Greeks, were ordered into Greece from Bulgaria to throw the British back into the sea. Hitler then ordered major units into northern Albania. This eccentric operation could have thrown into jeopardy any lightning success against Greece. But Hitler refused to give up his plan and his political will overrode all military objections. No harm was done, however, as the German High Command evaded executing the order, and events proved that they were right."

War in the mountains

Before Cavallero could meet the Duce's wishes he had to prevent the Greeks reaching Valona and Durazzo. At this date, to cover a front of 156 miles, he had 16 divisions, some in very bad shape and most of them poorly supplied on account of Albania's virtually non-existent communications. It is true that the opposing forces, the Greeks, who had been on the offensive since November 14, had lost a fair number of men and had only 13 divisions or their equivalent. Until such time as they could make up their strength and repair communications, General Papagos decided to abandon temporarily any idea of an all-out attack and restricted himself to limited-objective offensives. It was during one of these operations that the Greek II Corps, working as usual in the mountains, captured the important crossroads at Klisura on January 9. In a heavy snowstorm they inflicted a severe defeat on the "Lupi di Toscana" (Wolves of Tuscany) Division (General Ottavio Bollea), which had been force-marched to its objective. Papagos grouped his I and II Corps together under General Drakos as the Army of Epirus, but this was defeated at Telepenë in February. Not that the Greek troops lacked keenness or endurance (in his diary Cavallero says that their attacks were "frenzied"): they simply had no means of waging modern offensive warfare. This is clearly explained in the former Greek Commander-in-Chief's book on his army's operations:

British evacuation from Greece.

"The presence among the Italian troops of a considerable number of tanks, and the fact that we had none at all and very few anti-tank guns, forced us to keep well clear of the plains, which would allow rapid movement, and to manoeuvre only in the mountains. This increased the fatigue of the men and the beasts of burden, lengthened and delayed our convoys and brought additional difficulties in command, supplies and so on. The enemy, on the other hand, thanks to the means at his disposal, was able to fall back rapidly on the plains and take up new positions without much difficulty. Taking advantage of the terrain, he was then able to hold up our advance in the mountains with a relatively small number of men. Also, the fresh troops which the Italians brought up during this phase of the war came to the front in lorries, whereas ours had to move on foot, reaching the front tired and frequently too late to be of any use. As a final point I must mention the difficulties we had in restoring the works of art which had been damaged by the enemy, and the superiority of the Italian Air Force which, after the limited daily sorties by Greek and British planes, were able to attack with impunity both our forward and our rear areas." General Cavallero's success in these defensive operations gave him enough respite to reinforce and rest his troops so as to go over to the offensive as Mussolini had ordered.

From December 29, 1940, to March 26, 1941, no fewer than ten divisions, four machine gun battalions, together with

German troops with anti-aircraft gun.

that all the Albanian ports together, whatever might be done to increase their capacity, could only handle 4,000 tons a day? One of the few units lost during these operations was the hospital ship Po, torpedoed in error in Valona harbour. Countess Edda Ciano, who was serving on board as a nurse, escaped with no more than a ducking.

General Alexander Papagos was born in 1883, and was Commander-in-Chief of the Greek forces when Italy invaded Greece on October 28, 1940. Papagos's forces not only repulsed the Italians, but also counter-attacked into Albania. His forces held the renewed Italian offensive in March 1940, but the German offensive proved too much for them in April. He was arrested and taken to Germany, where he was freed by the Americans in 1945.

Another Italian offensive

three legions and 17 battalions of Black Shirts crossed the Adriatic. When spring came the Italian land forces in Albania thus comprised: the 9th and the 11th Armies, the 9th now under General Pirzio-Biroli and the 11th still under General Geloso: six corps, with 21 infantry divisions, five mountain divisions and the "Centauro" Armoured Division. The Greeks, on the other hand, had only 13 to 14 divisions, all of them suffering from battle fatigue.

This goes to show that, though denied the Mediterranean, the Italian Navy still controlled the Adriatic. Only one difficulty faced General Cavallero: was he to give priority to bringing up reinforcements or to supplying his troops at the front, given

As he had re-established numerical superiority, General Cavallero now set about his offensive operations. On March 9, 1941, watched by Mussolini, the 9th Army began attacking in the sector between the river Osum (called the Apsos by the Greeks) in the north-east and the Vijosë or the Aóos in the south-west. The area is dominated by the Trebesina mountains. General Geloso put in his IV, VIII and XXV Corps (Generals Mercalli, Gambara and Carlo Rossi respectively), comprising 11 infantry divisions and the "Centauro" Armoured Division. On D-day the Greeks had three divisions and the equivalent of a fourth, all from the II Corps (General Papadopoulos). At dawn the Greek positions were heavily shelled and bombed. From their observation point, at 0830, Mussolini and Cavallero could see the infantry moving up to their objectives over territory not unlike the Carso, where so many Italians had fallen in fruitless attacks between June 1915 and August 1917 during the First World War.

The Trebesina offensive did not restore the Duce's prestige. Not because the Greek defenders equalled the Italian attacking force in strength, as Cavallero wrote in his diary in the evening of March 9, but because they were well organised and their morale was high. He went on:

"The Greek artillery is powerfully deployed. All the elements of the defending forces are well organised in depth, using positions of strength which enable them to contain the offensive and to counterattack immediately and vigorously."

Forty-eight hours later, not only had there not been the expected breakthrough, but losses were mounting, the 11th Alpini Regiment alone reporting 356 killed and wounded, including 36 officers. Should the plan be abandoned after this discouraging start? Mussolini did not think so. That very day he said to General Geloso: "The directives of the plan must be adhered to at all costs. Between now and the end of the month a military victory is vital for the prestige of the Italian Army."

And he added, with an unusual disregard for his responsibilities in the matter of Italian military unpreparedness:

"I have always done my best to maintain the fame and the prestige of the Italian Army, but today it is vital to drive on with the offensive." They drove on, therefore, but attacks were followed by counterattacks and General Papagos having, so to speak, thrown two divisions into the fray, the Italians were no

further forward on the 15th than they had been on the 9th. When General Gambara was asked by Mussolini about the morale of his corps he replied, tactfully: "It cannot be said to be very high, but it remains firm. Losses, no territorial gains, few prisoners; this is hardly encouraging. All the same, morale is good enough not to prejudice the men's use in battle."

Mussolini and Cavallero finally drew the right conclusions from the situation and called off the attack. Mussolini returned to Rome without increasing his reputation. The three corps engaged in this unhappy affair lost 12,000 dead and wounded, or some 1,000 men per division. When it is realised that most of these losses were borne by the infantry it cannot be denied that they fought manfully.

The Greeks, on their side, however, suffered enormously and this defensive success, however honourable it might have been for their army, left them with only 14 divisions against 27.

Britain aids Greece

Meanwhile, on January 29, 1941, General Metaxas, who had forged the victories in Epirus and Albania, died suddenly in Athens and King George nominated Petros Koryzis as his successor. Events were soon to bring tragic proof that the new Greek Prime Minister could not match his predecessor in strength of character. He was, however, no less resolved to oppose with force the Germans' aggressive intentions in Rumania, as he made known in a letter to London dated February 8. This led to the departure from Plymouth on the 14th in a Sunderland flying boat bound for Cairo of Anthony Eden and Dill, the Chief of the

Imperial General Staff. General Wavell raised no objections in principle to aid for Greece, in spite of the serious risks involved. Eden was thus in a position to cable the Prime Minister on February 21:

"Dill and I have exhaustively reviewed situation temporarily [sic] with Commanders-in-Chief. Wavell is ready to make available three divisions, a Polish brigade and best part of an armoured division, together with a number of specialized troops such as anti-tank and anti-aircraft units. Though some of these … have yet to be concentrated, work is already in hand and they can reach Greece as rapidly as provision of ships will allow. This programme fulfils the hopes expressed at Defence Committee that we could make available a force of three divisions and an armoured division.

"Gravest anxiety is not in respect of army but of air. There is no doubt that need to fight a German air force, instead of Italian, is creating a new problem for Longmore. My own impression is that all his squadrons are not quite up to standard of their counterpart at home ….. We should all have liked to approach Greeks tomorrow with a suggestion that we should join with them in holding a line to defend Salonika, but both Longmore and Cunningham are convinced that our present air resources will not allow us to do this ."

The truth is that the R.A.F. would find itself having to face not the Italian Air Force but the Luftwaffe, and that is why both Air Chief-Marshal Longmore and Admiral Cunningham doubted if the expeditionary force could fight on a front covering Salonika. These doubts were shared also by Sir John Dill. However, the matter was to be discussed with the Greeks at a secret conference on the following day (February 22) at the Royal Palace at Tatoi, near Athens. The results were to prove very dangerous.

General Count Ugo Cavallero, born in 1880, was appointed Under-Secretary of War by Mussolini in 1925 and later became Chief-of-Staff to the Duke of Aosta in Abyssinia. He became Chief of the Italian General Staff on Badoglio's resignation in 1940, a post which he held until Mussolini's overthrow in 1943. After a spell in prison he was released, but committed suicide shortly afterwards.

The Greek viewpoint

The conference was attended by King George II, Anthony Eden, Prime Minister Koryzis, the British Ambassador in Athens, Generals Dill and Wavell, Air Chief-Marshal Longmore, and the heads of the British Military Missions in Greece. General Papagos was asked to report on the latest situation.

After giving an account of the latest Intelligence information, he put forward the solution he would advocate if Yugoslavia were to remain neutral and refuse to allow German troops to cross her territory. In this hypothesis the defence of western Thrace and eastern Macedonia would seem to be inadvisable. 'Troops defending the Metaxas Line, the main bulwark against Bulgaria, would therefore be given the task of slowing down the enemy advance, holding out to the last round, but the troops supporting them opposite Yugoslavia (three divisions) would fall back on a position between the lower Aliákmon river and the Vérmion and Kaïmakchalán mountains, which rise, respectively, to 6,725 and

8,375 feet. If all went well this operation should take about 20 days. But Papagos thought that the German forces in Rumania would need only a fortnight to get to the Bulgarian-Greek frontier from the left bank of the Danube.

Bulgaria joins the Tripartite Pact

On March 1, 1941 Bulgaria joined the Tripartite Pact and the German 12th Army under Field-Marshal List crossed the Danube on pontoon bridges. In line with undertakings given on the previous January 18, this event decided the Athens Government to allow the entry into Greece of the expeditionary force organised in Cairo and put under the command of Sir Henry Maitland Wilson. But however strongly the British might have insisted, General Papagos refused to begin the anticipated withdrawal from Thrace and eastern Macedonia. It was already March 4 and everything inclined to the belief that if his three divisions on the Metaxas Line were given the order, they would now be caught in full movement.

From March 7 onwards the British Expeditionary Force began to land at the ports of Piraeus and Vólos. It was transported in 25 ships and no untoward incident occurred, as the Italian air forces based in the Dodecanese were not up to strength. Altogether 57,577 men and about 100 tanks were landed to form the 1st Armoured Brigade, the 6th Australian Division (Maj.-Gen. Sir Iven Mackay) and the 2nd New Zealand Division, the latter being under Major-General Bernard Freyberg, V.C., a hero of the Dardanelles and the Somme.

At the end of the month Maitland Wilson's troops were in

German tanks enter Belgrade.

position behind the Aliákmon and the Vérmion mountains. On the other hand, after negotiations which, in a telegram dated March 4, Eden describes somewhat testily as "bargaining more reminiscent of oriental bazaars", the Greek High Command put under the B.E.F. three divisions (the 12th, the 20th, and the 19th Motorised) with seven battalions withdrawn from the Turkish border after reassurances from Ankara. The British expected more of their allies, but it should be noted on the other hand, that the 7th Australian Division (Major-General J. D. Lavarack) and the 1st Polish Brigade (General Kopanski), which should have been sent to Greece, never left the Middle East.

German SS Leibstandarte on parade.

The Battle of Matapan

In the afternoon of March 27 a Sunderland flying boat spotted the squadron, which was then steaming through the Ionian Sea. The British had thus been alerted, as decoded messages subsequently confirmed, and it was now unlikely that any of their convoys could be intercepted. Yet the only offensive orders countermanded by Supermarina were those concerning the area north of Crete. That same evening Cunningham slipped out of Alexandria with three battleships and the aircraft-carrier Formidable, which had 37 aircraft on board. He had arranged a rendezvous south-east of Gávdhos with Vice-Admiral H. D. Pridham-Wippell's squadron of four cruisers from Piraeus.

First contact, at about 0800 hours, was between Admiral Sansonetti's three heavy cruisers and Pridham-Wippell's light cruisers. Though the British ships mounted only 6-inch guns against the Italian vessels' 8-inchers, their evasive action, contrary to the Royal Navy's tradition of aggressiveness; led Iachino to think that they might be acting as bait for a large ship as yet out of sight. He therefore recalled Sansonetti. Pridham-Wippell then gave chase, only to find himself being fired on by the Vittorio

Veneto's 15-inch guns. The Italians loosed off 94 rounds but failed to score a hit. Then at about mid-day torpedo-carrying aircraft from the Formidable launched a first attack, but without success. Admiral Iachino thereupon headed back to base.

At 1510 hours, the Fleet Air Arm launched its second attack. At the cost of his life, Lieutenant-Commander J. Dalyell-Stead dropped his torpedo at very short range and severely damaged the Vittorio Veneto, causing her to ship 4,000 tons of water and putting her two port engines out of action. Thanks to the efforts of her crew the damaged battleship got under way again at a speed of first 17, then 19 knots.

By this time Cunningham, with the main body of his fleet, was about 87 miles away. The Formidable's planes kept him fully informed of the Italian movements, whereas Iachino was in complete ignorance of Cunningham's, and was no better informed than he had been defended by the exiguous Axis air support. In des pair, and relying on a radio bearing from Supermarina, Iachino admitted that he was being chased by an aircraft-carrier and a cruiser some 170 miles away.

As daylight faded he gathered about the damaged flagship his 1st and 3rd Cruiser Squadrons and the destroyers in case another attack was made by British aircraft. These had, in fact, been ordered to delay the Vittorio Veneto so that the British battleships could finish her off. Iachino's defensive tactics, including the use of smoke screens, prevented this, but towards 1925 hours the heavy cruiser Pola was torpedoed. Iachino ordered Admiral Cattaneo to stay with the Pola, taking her in tow if possible and scuttling her if this proved impracticable. The decision was later criticised, but was justified in the light of Iachino's estimate of the British position. However this may be, the luckless cruiser then came up on the Ajax's radar screen. Pridham-Wippell took her for the Vittorio Veneto and signalled to Cunningham, who was closing with the Warspite, Valiant, and Barham. At about 2200 hours Valiant's radar picked up Cattaneo's cruisers sailing blindly forward into the darkness. Some 30 minutes later the British squadron's 24 15-inch guns blasted them out of the water at point-blank range. The Fiume went down at 2315 hours, the Zara, which was sinking more slowly, was scuttled by her commander and the destroyers Alfieri and Carducci met a similar fate. Finally a British destroyer sank Pola after picking up her survivors.

That night and the morning after the battle, which took place 112 miles southwest of Cape Matapan, the British, with the aid of some Greek destroyers, picked up just over a thousand survivors. The rescue operations were hampered by a Luftwaffe attack, but Cunningham generously signalled Rome, giving the area where further survivors might still be found. The hospital ship Gradisca subsequently picked up another 160. Altogether 2,400 Italian seamen were lost, including Admiral Cattaneo and the commanders of the cruisers Zara and Fiume, Captains Giorgis and Corsi respectively. The only British loss was that of the heroic Dalyell-Stead.

Although Admiral Cunningham was not altogether satisfied with the outcome of the battle, since the Vittorio Veneto had got away and reached Taranto, Cape Matapan was a heavy defeat for the Italian Navy, which had lost at one blow three of its 12,000-ton cruisers, a loss which could not be made good overnight. This was what Mussolini had in mind when he received Admiral Iachino at the Palazzo Venezia.

"The operation promised well and might have been successful had it not been for the total lack of co-operation from the air arm. During the whole time you never had a single Italian or German plane over you. All the aircraft you saw were the enemy's. They chased you, attacked you, overpowered you. Your ships were like blind invalids being set upon by several armed killers."

Naval operations, then, were impossible in British-controlled waters without proper reconnaissance and fighter support. Mussolini concluded, with what Iachino describes as the true journalist's capacity for summing things up: "And as fighter aircraft have a limited range, the ships must take their escorts with them. In a word, all naval forces must always be accompanied by at least one aircraft-carrier."

And so, the Duce was going back on the point of view he had expressed in 1930, but rather belatedly, after a defeat which weighed heavily on Italian strategy. To alleviate the consequences it was decided to convert two liners, Roma and Augustus, into aircraft-carriers and rename them Aquila and Sparviero. Until they came into service the fleet was forbidden to sail outside land-based fighter range.

The exploit of Lieutenant Faggioni and his five men in the battle of Cape Matapan deserves not to be forgotten. During the night of March 25–26 they managed to get into Suda Bay, on the north coast of Crete, in boats loaded with explosives. There they effectively crippled the cruiser York and the oil-tanker Pericles.

German assault - paras drop from junkers, one on fire.

With Greece evacuated, should the Allies have continued to cling on to Crete? British critics of Churchill's war strategy have said on more than one occasion that the island should have been abandoned. Yet a glance at the map will show that whereas Crete is 500 miles from Alexandria, it is only 200 from Tobruk. Tobruk, the bastion of British resistance in the Middle East, could only be supplied by sea and the great danger was that it might be starved out if the Luftwaffe controlled the aerodromes at Máleme and Heraklion. If Churchill is to be criticised for wanting to fight the war on every front with insufficient means, this is not a front which should be held against him.

Hitler drew similar conclusions. His aims were defensive as well as offensive. Within a few weeks the unleashing of "Barbarossa" would deprive him (only temporarily he hoped) of

Russian oil. What would happen if the R.A.F. on Crete were to wipe out all the production of Ploie ti? That is why, on April 25, 1941, his Directive No. 28 ordered the three armies in Greece to prepare Operation "Mercury", which was to secure Crete for Germany.

Brauchitsch, Göring, and Raeder set to work with great energy. And it was no small matter to plan an operation of the size required in a country with such limited resources as Greece where, in particular, air bases had to be improvised.

German paratroops land

The German invasion of Crete began early on May 20, when airborne troops of the 7th Fliegerdivision were dropped around Máleme, Réthimnon and Heraklion. The defenders had been expecting them for 48 hours and so the fighting was bitter. At Máleme General Meindl, gravely wounded, had to hand over his command to Colonel Ramcke; at Réthimnon the paratroops landed with no commander at all as the glider carrying General Sussman had crashed on the island of Aegina. The battle might have swung in General Freyberg's favour had he had time to reinforce the brigade defending Máleme airstrip against Ramcke, and if the Mediterranean Fleet had been able to destroy completely the convoys bringing in Lieutenant-General Ringel's mountain troops. But, for the few losses they inflicted on the Germans, the Royal Navy lost, in rapid succession from aerial bombardment by Stukas, the cruisers Gloucester and Fiji together with four destroyers, while the Warspite and the aircraft-carrier Formidable were so badly damaged that they had to be sent for

repair in the United States.

In spite of pressure from London, Admiral Cunningham had to give up operations north of Crete, where he was suffering heavy losses. On May 25, with admirably controlled air support, the 5th Mountain Division managed to break out of the Máleme perimeter held by the 2nd New Zealand Division and push on through Canea. The German breakthrough decided General Freyberg on May 27 to begin the evacuation of the island and to ask for help from the Mediterranean Fleet. This help was not refused him.

The evacuation of Crete

In spite of the risks involved and the losses already sustained, the Commander-in-Chief Mediterranean, Admiral Cunningham, did not hesitate a moment.

"We cannot let [the army] down," he signalled to the ships of his fleet which had been designated for this mission, and when one member of his staff seemed pessimistic he retorted, with a just sense of realities: "It takes the Navy three years to build a ship. It would take 300 years to re-build a tradition."

The evacuation of Crete, begun on the night of May 28–29, was carried out through the small harbour at Sphakia on the south coast and was completed by dawn on June 2. During the operation the A.A. cruiser Calcutta and the destroyers Hereward and Imperial were lost. But the heaviest losses of life were on board the cruiser Orion, Vice-Admiral Pridham Wippell's flagship. One single German bomb killed 260 men and wounded 280.

British Empire losses were nearly 1,800 killed and about

General Student and members of a parachute reg plan their next move.

German paratroopers resting in Greece.

12,000 captured out of 32,000 men engaged. The Royal Navy lost 1,828 killed and 183 wounded. 18,000 troops were evacuated to Egypt. But the losses of General Student and XI Fliegerkorps had not been slight in spite of this. Though the Germans' casualties could not have reached the 15,000 given by Churchill in his memoirs, statistics published since the war show that, with 3,714 killed and missing and 2,494 wounded, the eight days of fighting on Crete had cost the Germans, particularly in the loss of experienced airborne troops, more than the whole three weeks of the Balkans campaign.

Was it because of these German losses that Hitler rejected General Student's suggestion to follow up the victory on Crete by capturing Cyprus? We do not know. But the memory of this blood-bath admittedly encouraged Hitler to abandon his operation "Hercules" (the capture of Malta from the air) in late June 1942, when Rommel thought he had convinced him that the Axis forces could get to the Nile and Suez. In any case, the British forces in Libya, in Macedonia, and in the Aegean Sea had suffered heavy reverses which more than balanced the losses accountable to Italian strategy in the previous winter. Did the War Cabinet's decisions and the orders of the Imperial General Staff "lamentably" fail to appreciate the situation, as Lord Cunningham of Hyndhope claims in his A Sailor's Odyssey? It is difficult to dispute the validity of this statement by one of the great commanders of the war, yet in the end, we cannot always do as we would wish in war and sometimes the only choice left lies between two very great disadvantages. Churchill's solution was not necessarily the wrong one, therefore. Fifteen years of disarmament had reduced Britain to this level of impotence.

British Crusader tanks in formation.

Until Pearl Harbor, developments in the North African campaign depended on the course of the naval/air war in the Mediterranean. This was affected to a great extent by the defensive and offensive capabilities of Malta, which relied on supplies sent from England and Egypt. It was a case of "triphibious" warfare, as Winston Churchill called it. The Italian Navy, whose task was to keep open the sealanes to the forces fighting in Libya and Egypt, was faced, from mid-July 1941, with an increasingly difficult situation. Already at a disadvantage as it lacked any naval airpower worthy of the name, its shortage of oil fuel was now assuming tragic proportions. It had entered the war with reserves of 1,880,000 tons, 600,000 of which had been consumed in the first six months of operations. Monthly consumption was reduced to 75,000 tons. But when it became clear that supplies from Germany would not exceed 50,000 tons a month, this meant, recorded Supermarina, that it would be impossible "to maintain forces in a state that was already inadequate for waging war".

But even these supplies could not be relied on, for when the yearly figures were established it was shown that supplies from Germany amounted to barely 254,000 tons, instead of the 600,000 tons expected. One can understand why, just before El Alamein, the Chief-of-Staff of the Italian Comando Supremo, Marshal Cavallero, wrote in his diary on October 23, 1942: "I have two major preoccupations — oil and Malta."

Thus it is clear that in this and many other respects Operation "Barbarossa" damaged the Axis potential in the Mediterranean.

The success of Operation "Tiger"

The arrival in Africa of the 15th Panzer Division in the latter part of April caused alarm in G.H.Q. Cairo and in the British War Cabinet. General Wavell expected a strong force of German infantry to move up the line, and on April 20 he signalled to the C.I.G.S., Sir John Dill:

"I have just received disquieting intelligence. I was expecting another German colonial division, which disembarked at Tripoli early this month, to appear in the fighting line about the end of the month. Certain units have already been identified. I have just been informed that latest evidence indicates this is not a colonial but an armoured division. If so, the situation is indeed serious, since an armoured division contains over 400 tanks, of which 138 are medium. If the enemy can arrange supply it will take a lot of stopping."

It is now known that Wavell over estimated considerably the strength of the Panzer division in the spring of 1941. Instead of the three or four tank battalions at the disposal of the large armoured units in action in the Balkans at this time, the 15th Panzer Division had only two, which comprised 168 tanks and 30 reconnaissance vehicles. It must be recognised, however, that this distinguished soldier was basing his assessment on reports not only from the British Intelligence service but also from its French, Belgian, and Swiss counterparts. These sources gave the Panzer strength as 488, including 122 heavy tanks.

In any case, once he had "digested" the information, Wavell informed Dill that he attached the highest priority to immediate reinforcement of his armoured strength. He had in reserve sufficient personnel to man six armoured regiments, and was insistent that the tanks he needed should be delivered before the 15th Panzer Division was in position and ready for action. Churchill overruled the objections of the C.I.G.S., who was reluctant to weaken the home front while there was still a possibility of a German invasion, excluded the Cape route in view of the urgency of the problem, and insisted that the First Lord of the Admiralty order delivery by the Mediterranean route. At the same time, the battleship Queen Elizabeth and the cruisers Fiji and Naiad were transferred from home waters to Alexandria. Two hundred and ninety-five tanks and 53 Hurricane fighters were loaded aboard five fast 15-knot merchant ships.

This convoy was escorted by Force H between Gibraltar and Cape Bon. During the night of May 7–8 one merchant ship struck a mine in the dangerous Sicilian Narrows, but the next day, 55 miles south of Malta, the convoy was taken over by Admiral Cunningham who, while he was about it, shelled Benghazi and sent three tankers and four supply ships to Malta. A few days later, the four remaining ships unloaded at Alexandria 43 Hurricanes and 238 tanks — 135 Matildas, 82 cruisers, and 21 Mark VI's, small 5½-ton machines of relatively little value in battle. Apparently, the transfer of X Fliegerkorps from Sicily to Rommel in Africa had contributed considerably to the success of this daring operation — "Tiger" as it was named by Churchill.

Indian troops clearing a village with a Bren Gun carrier.

Rommel maintains his advantage

The War Cabinet had learned from intercepts of "Enigma" signals that Rommel had various weaknesses. Wavell was therefore urged to attack with minimum delay, and to relieve the tired garrison of Tobruk. He had under his command XIII Corps, under Lieutenant-General Sir Noel Beresford-Peirse, including the 4th Indian Division (Major-General F. W. Messervy), the 7th Armoured Division (Major-General Sir Michael O'Moore Creagh), and the 22nd Guards Brigade (Brigadier J. Marriot).

However, recent engagements at Halfaya Pass had made him aware of a number of "black spots". In a message to the C.I.G.S. on May 28 he said:

"Our armoured cars are too lightly armoured to resist the fire of enemy fighter aircraft, and, having no gun, are powerless against the German eight-wheeled armoured cars, which have guns and are faster. This makes reconnaissance difficult. Our Infantry tanks are really too slow for a battle in desert, and have been suffering considerable casualties from the fire of the powerful enemy anti-tank guns. Our cruisers have little advantage in power or speed over German medium tanks. Technical breakdowns are still too numerous. We shall not be able to accept battle with perfect confidence in spite of numerical inferiority, as we could against Italians. Above factors may limit our success. They also make it imperative that adequate flow of armoured reinforcements and reserves should be maintained."

Did General Wavell exaggerate the weakness of his armoured forces? It is unlikely, since Rommel's account completely supports Wavell. Discussing his successful defensive action of June 15–17, 1941, Rommel wrote:

"But [Wavell] was put at a great disadvantage by the slow speed of his heavy Infantry tanks, which prevented him from reacting quickly enough to the moves of our faster vehicles. Hence the slow speed of the bulk of his armour was his soft spot, which we could seek to exploit tactically."

He also reveals that the Matilda tanks, which were supposed to sweep a path for the infantry through enemy defences, had only anti-tank armour-piercing shells.

Against troops that were widely spread and well dug in one might as well have used the iron cannon ball of the Napoleonic wars. Finally, the Afrika Korps' commander used 8.8-cm anti-aircraft guns as anti-tank weapons. This 21-pounder gun was highly accurate, firing 15 to 20 rounds a minute at a velocity of over 2,600 feet per second. It thus outclassed all British armour, which could be knocked out even before the Germans were within range of their 40-mm guns. After the battle the British said they had been taken by surprise, but it was really nothing new. Colonel de Gaulle had been through the experience at the Abbeville bridgehead on May 30, 1940.

In these circumstances it was not surprising that the British offensive, Operation "Battleaxe", was a failure. Wavell had not even had the advantage of surprise. The plan was to take the Halfaya position in an encircling movement, with the 7th Armoured Division attacking the rear and the 4th Indian Division making the frontal assault. After an initial success by the 7th Armoured Division, which took Capuzzo, the whole operation went wrong.

For one thing, General Beresford-Peirse's command was apparently too remote and inflexible. Also, at Halfaya Pass, the battalion of the 15th Panzer holding the position put up a remarkable fight although almost completely surrounded. Its commander, Captain Wilhelm Bach, formerly a priest in Baden and conscripted in 1939, aided by Major Pardi of the Italian artillery, offered a determined and courageous resistance. Their gallantry gave Rommel the time to bring the whole of his forces to bear. By June 16 he had stabilised the situation, bringing the British to a halt with considerable casualties. But he was not the man to be satisfied with a merely defensive success. Assembling as much of his Afrika Korps as possible he struck south, reaching Sidi Omar, then east, hoping to surround and wipe out XIII Corps. The British managed to withdraw, however, before their last lines of communication were cut, and on June 17 all was quiet again on the Halfaya escarpment.

Of the 25,000 men in the engagement, British casualties were 122 killed, 588 wounded, and 259 missing, most of whom were taken prisoner. Wavell's fears on May 28 were justified if one considers the losses in his armoured units. Of the 180 tanks which had set off at dawn on June 15, about 100 were lost. As for Rommel, he recorded the loss of 12 tanks totally destroyed and 675 men, including 338 dead or missing. His success was timely as he had many critics in O.K.H. and especially since on June 22 O.K.W. was to assume complete control over this theatre of operations.

Auchinleck replaces Wavell

The defeat of XIII Corps at Halfaya led to the removal of its commander. In London, Churchill decided that the G.H.Q. Cairo needed new inspiration and strength and so replaced Wavell by General Sir Claude Auchinleck, formerly Commander-in-Chief, India. Was Wavell really "exhausted", as Churchill claimed? He certainly had more responsibilities than he would have liked, in view of the lack of resources at his disposal. But nevertheless his successor, who took over on July 5, later told the British historian Correlli Barnett: "Wavell showed no signs of tiredness at all. He was always the same. I think he was first class; in spite of his silences, he made a tremendous impact on his troops. I have a very great admiration for him … but he was given impossible tasks."

Perhaps it should be noted that Auchinleck, after his own misfortune in 1942, was not enamoured of Churchill. And Sir Alan Brooke, C.-in-C., Home Forces, wrote in his diary on June 17, 1941 that he entirely disapproved of Churchill's strategy:

"The P.M. began with a survey of the world situation which was interesting. To my horror he informed us that the present Libyan operation is intended to be a large-scale operation! How can we undertake offensive operations on two fronts in the Middle East when we have not got sufficient for one? From the moment we decided to go into Syria we should have put all our strength in the front to complete the operation with the least possible delay. If the operation is not pressed through quickly, it may well lead to further complications."

In fact, Wavell's thinking corresponded exactly with Brooke's concerning orders to move troops to various foreign theatres (Balkans, Crete, Iraq, and Syria), with complete disregard for the principle of concentration of force, as applied in the main areas of Tobruk and Halfaya. Whereas Brooke could only write in his diary at his London H.Q. in St. Paul's School, Wavell would have been failing in his duty as commanding officer if he had not put before Churchill all the dangers involved in the latter's strategy. This is exactly what he did, even offering to resign, in the hope of calling off the operation intended to win Syria from the Vichy régime. At the same time he was ordered to speed up preparations for "Battleaxe", of which the government expected no less than the rapid destruction of the Afrika Korps. As we know, Wavell finally gave in to Churchill and launched the operation, although disapproving of it in principle. His professional military judgement was, however, entirely vindicated.

It is worth noting that it took over a month for Lieutenant-General Maitland Wilson to overcome the resistance of General Henri Dentz who, in any case, had no intention of fighting to the last man. But the two divisions employed in this Syrian operation could well have been employed in the Western Desert. What would have happened if they had been in position at Sidi Omar to face Rommel? It is, of course, a matter of conjecture, but Rommel's flanking tactics on June 16 and 17 might have ended in failure.

Air Chief Marshal Longmore, commanding the British air forces in the Middle East, was recalled to London and was then given the post of Inspector-General of the R.A.F. His place was taken by Air-Marshal Sir Arthur Tedder, later chosen by Eisenhower to be his Deputy C.-in-C. just before the Normandy landings. Also, the War Cabinet appointed Oliver Lyttelton, formerly President of the Board of Trade, as resident Minister of State in the Middle East. More fortunate than his predecessor, General Auchinleck, relieved of a host of political and administrative duties, was to be able to devote himself entirely to military matters in his own province.

Before examining Auchinleck's operations, we should look briefly at events in Iraq and Syria.

The Iraqi rebellion

At the end of March 1941, the Emir Abdul Illah, Regent of Iraq and a strong supporter of friendship with Britain, had to leave his capital after a rebellion by his premier, Rashid Ali,

Light tanks, guns, rifles, lorries, which were captured when the British took Agordat.

and a mutiny in the army. On May 2 his partisans attacked Habbāniyah, the large air base on the right bank of the Euphrates some 30 miles from Baghdad. Were the rebels going to cut the pipeline taking oil from the Mosul fields to Haifa? Were they going to occupy Basra, within reach of the Kuwait oil wells and the Abadan refinery? It was a critical time for the British, but the events seemed to have taken both Hitler and Mussolini by surprise. Not until May 23 did the Führer sign his Directive Number 30, ordering the organisation and despatch to Baghdad of a military mission commanded by General Hellmuth Felmy. Its

task was to prepare for action a unit each of Messerschmitt Bf 109 fighters and of Heinkel He 111 bombers. Mussolini's contribution was a promise to send a few fighters to Iraq.

But by this time Churchill had already seized the initiative. He was aware of Wavell's doubts in Cairo, but in India the Viceroy, Lord Linlithgow, and General Auchinleck diverted to Basra an Indian division previously intended for Malaya. On May 19 a motorised division from Palestine arrived at Habbāniyah, where the rebel siege had been abandoned. On the rebels' surrender, a cease-fire was declared on May 30, and Rashid Ali left for Germany, by way of Iraq and Turkey.

An enormous pile of captured Italian rifles

General Sir Claude Auchinleck had commanded in northern Norway during the abortive campaign of spring 1940. After a spell as G.O.C., Southern Command, in England, he went to India as C.-in-C. in 1941. His prompt despatch of an Indian division to help put down the Iraqi revolt earned him Churchill's approval, and he was the man selected by Churchill to replace Wavell in late June 1941. After settling the problem posed by Vichy Syria, Auchinleck turned to the paramount task of beating Rommel in the Western Desert and resuming the advance on Tripoli begun with so much promise by "Wavell's Thirty Thousand" in December 1940. Forced by his other heavy duties to work from Cairo, he did not hesitate to fly up to the front and take over personal control when the 8th Army found itself in trouble - as it did during "Crusader", its first offensive, in November 1941. But he fell foul of Churchill and was replaced in August 1942.

Surrender at Acre

On July 10 Dentz, who had lost 6,500 men, most of his aircraft, the destroyer Chevalier Paul and the submarine Souffleur, sent General de Verdillac to Maitland Wilson, who offered the French representative very honourable terms. The surrender agreement was signed at Acre on July 14, but not without vigorous protest from General de Gaulle, who considered that he had been cheated of his share of the victory. An addition to the agreement, on July 24, gave him the right to the French forces' equipment in the Levant and facilities for recruiting among the 30,000 men who had surrendered. One hundred and twenty-seven officers and 6,000 men were thus induced to join de Gaulle's Free French forces. Writing of this division among the beaten French, de Gaulle said:

"But 25,000 officers, N.C.O.s and men of the French Army and Air Force were finally torn away from us, whereas the great majority would without any doubt have decided to join us if we had had the time to enlighten them. For those Frenchmen who were returning to France with the permission of the enemy, so giving up the possibility of returning there as fighters, were, I knew, submerged in doubt and sadness. As for me, it was with my heart wrung that I gazed at the Vichy transports lying in the harbour and saw them, once loaded, disappear out to sea, taking with them one of the chances of our country."

General de Gaulle had appointed General Catroux his "Delegate-General and Plenipotentiary in the Levant", giving him instructions to negotiate, with the Syrian and Lebanese authorities, a new statute granting the two countries independence and sovereignty but ensuring that they remained allies of France. But propaganda, intrigues and money were already being employed by, among others, Glubb "Pasha" at Palmyra, Commodore Bass in the Jebel ed Draz, arid the chief British liaison officer, General Spears, at Damascus and Beirat to supplant Vichy and Free France alike. This caused new quarrels between Oliver Lyttelton and General de Gaulle. But there was nothing the French could do to prevent the appointment, in January 1942, of General Spears as Minister Plenipotentiary in Syria and the Lebanon. Spears was a former friend of de Gaulle and there is little doubt that what he had to do was not his own personal responsibility but attributable to the Prime Minister and Anthony Eden. In 1945 it was thought in London that the celebrated Colonel T. E. Lawrence's dream of undivided British influence throughout the Arab world was about to become a reality. It did not take long for events to prove that there was no substance in this dream.

Relations between the new C.-in-C. Middle East and Churchill differed very little from those in Wavell's time. On his arrival in Cairo on July 1, Auchinleck received a letter from Churchill apparently giving him complete freedom of action in his own sphere of responsibility. But this was no more than a façade; Churchill neither expected the C.-in-C. in Cairo to have any other criteria with which to judge the situation than those applied in Downing Street, nor did he envisage any other plans than his own.

And no sooner had Auchinleck demanded three months of preparations and three or four extra divisions (two or three of them armoured), than these two equally determined men found themselves in violent disagreement. At the end of July, Auchinleck was summoned to London to explain his views. His arguments were sound enough to win over the General Staff and the War Cabinet, but, as Churchill's memoirs show, he did not alter the Prime Minister's basic convictions. Nevertheless, Churchill had to bow to the majority and accept that Operation "Crusader", aimed at expelling Rommel from Cyrenaica, should be postponed until the period between September 15 and November 1.

Australian infantry watch Italian troops.

Before zero hour on the desert front, the British and Australian Governments were involved in an incident with unfortunate consequences. Defeated in Parliament, Mr. Menzies' Liberal Government gave way to a Labour administration headed first by Mr. Fadden, then by Mr. Curtin. Australian opinion had become extremely sensitive following all kinds of alarmist rumours about Tobruk. Anxious to appease public feeling, the new cabinet demanded the immediate relief of the Australians in the garrison.

Whatever he said or did, the Prime Minister had to fall in with this demand, which was put forward in a most truculent manner, for however loyal the Dominions were to the United Kingdom, their relationship was between equals and decisions had to be negotiated, not imposed by Westminster.

Therefore, using periods of the new moon in September and October, a shuttle operation was organised, bringing into Tobruk General S. Kopanski's Polish 1st Carpathian Brigade and the British 70th Division, commanded by Major-General R. M. Scobie, and evacuating to Alexandria the 9th Australian Division and the 18th Australian Infantry Brigade Group. In spite of the loss of the fast minelayer Latona, the operation was completely successful.

Owing to the late arrival in Egypt of the 22nd Armoured Brigade, Auchinleck found that he was obliged to postpone his attack from November 1 to November 18. Churchill has been criticised for his irritation at the delay, but seen in the context of the overall situation, there was some rational justification on his side. He wanted Rommel attacked, beaten, and eliminated in Cyrenaica before a likely German victory in Russia permitted Hitler to drive his Panzers across the Caucasus towards the Persian Gulf and the Red Sea. This is precisely what the Wehrmacht was planning to do.

Malta reinforced

The new delay 'to "Crusader" had no adverse effect on the progress of the operations, thanks to the pressure exerted on Axis communications in the Mediterranean by the sea and naval air forces of Admirals Cunningham and Somerville. No harm can be done to these remarkable commanders' reputations by pointing out two circumstances which made their task easier. In the first place, after the Balkans campaign X Fliegerkorps did not return to its bases in Sicily but served with Rommel. In the second place, the Italian fleet was not permitted to operate beyond coastal waters. In these conditions, the three convoys sent to Malta during 1941 lost only one merchant ship out of the 40 which left Gibraltar. Force H came well out of these dangerous operations, losing only the cruiser Southampton and the destroyer Fearless, though the battleship Nelson was seriously damaged on the "Halberd" convoy in a torpedo attack by an audacious Italian pilot.

In the same period the aircraft-carrier Ark Royal, sometimes accompanied by the Victorious, despatched to Malta nearly 300 fighters, most of which reached their destination. Also, during the summer, the island's airfields were reoccupied by a small attacking force of Blenheim and Wellington bombers. Finally, on October 21, Captain W. G. Agnew's Force K-the light cruisers Aurora and Penelope, from Scapa Flow — anchored in the Grand Harbour. The situation around Malta now seemed sufficiently under control for the Admiralty to send the cruisers Ajax and Neptune to join them a few weeks later.

This succession of reinforcements explains why, from August onwards, supplies to the Axis forces in Libya became more and more unreliable. During September, 94,000 tons of equipment and fuel were loaded in Italy, but 26,000 tons of it went to the bottom. Submarines operating from Malta took the lion's share of this destruction. For example, on September 18 Commander Wanklyn in Upholder sank with five torpedoes the two 19,500 ton ships Oceania and Neptunia. Also taking part in this sea offensive were the Alexandria and Gibraltar flotillas, including two

An Axis airfield showing German Junkers JU52 planes.

Dutch vessels.

The Italian defence was at a disadvantage in this fighting since their vessels had no asdic of the type used by British escorts. A few dozen sets were obtained from Germany during the summer of 1941, but it took time for them to be installed and crews trained to use them, time which was not wasted by their opponents. On the other hand, minefields in waters around Malta and Tripoli accounted for five of the eight British submarines lost in the Mediterranean in 1941.

In October, losses of supplies between Italian ports and Tripolitania amounted to one fifth of the cargoes loaded, and of 12,000 tons of fuel bound for the Axis forces, 2,500 tons

Headquarters outside Bardia.

Trieste, and four destroyers). At 1645 the convoy was sighted and reported to Malta by a Maryland on patrol. At nightfall Captain Agnew set out with his cruisers and the destroyers Lance and Lively. Other aircraft, in constant radar contact with the enemy, guided him to the convoy.

Towards 0100, about 155 miles east of Syracuse, the convoy appeared on the radar screens of the British ships, themselves still unseen by the Italians. Less than ten minutes later it was all over, after a barrage of shellfire and torpedoes. The seven merchant ships were sinking, and the destroyer Fulmine was going down with them, shattered by a salvo from the Aurora. The attack had been so rapid that the 3rd Cruiser Squadron, in any case badly equipped for battle at night, had not time to intervene. On top of all this, near dawn, the destroyer Libeccio was sunk by the tireless Upholder.

With losses mounting, Supermarina tried to ensure delivery of the fuel vital to the Libyan operations by using very fast light cruisers. As a result of this decision, there was another disaster during the night of December 13. Loaded with drums of oil, the cruisers Alberico da Barbiano and Alberto di Guissano had sailed for Tripoli from Palermo. They were sighted by Malta-based aircraft which transmitted the information to Commander G. H. Stokes, leading four destroyers, including the Dutch vessel Isaac Sweers, from Gibraltar to Alexandria. Stokes surprised the two Italian ships off Cape Bon. Their cargo caught fire immediately and most of their crews, including Admiral Toscano, perished. And as if this were not enough, during the same night two brand new merchant ships, Filzi and Del Greco, were sunk.

disappeared into the sea. November was even worse, and for a while it was thought that Rommel would be brought to a standstill. In fact, out of a total of 79,208 tons of supplies loaded in Italy, he lost 62 per cent (49,365 tons). Every episode in the first battle of the convoys cannot be described here, but the disaster of November 9 does deserve mention in some detail.

Nine sinkings in ten minutes

The convoy "Duisburg", composed of six merchant ships and a tanker, left from Messina on the afternoon of November 8. It was closely escorted by six destroyers, backed up by the 3rd Cruiser Squadron commanded by Vice-Admiral Brivonesi (Trento,

In short, post-war statistics show that in the second half of 1941 Italy lost no less than 189 merchant vessels totalling 500,000 tons. On June 10, 1940, taking into account 500,000 tons of Italian shipping frozen in American ports, the Italian merchant fleet had totalled 3,300,000 tons. As a result of these losses, the situation for the Italians by the middle of December was, to say the least, very serious.

Was Supermarina betrayed?

When one considers these events, so disastrous for the Axis, the question arises whether they were due to treason committed by a member of Supermarina in a key position. This question caused violent arguments in Italy, and ended in the courts. In his book The Foxes of the Desert, Paul Carell supports this view, but such serious naval historians as Bragadin and Admiral Bernotti refute it. Methodical modern techniques of enquiry, using evidence from continuous monitoring of enemy radio communications, tend to leave one sceptical of the theory. Moreover, there were one or more British submarines permanently on the watch outside every port where convoys were formed. Finally, the two incidents already described are proof of the excellent work done by reconnaissance aircraft, operating from Malta with complete impunity.

Cavallero seeks to occupy Tunisia

Marshal Cavallero, Chief-of-Staff at Comando Supremo, had not waited until disaster was inevitable before grasping the importance of the port of Bizerta and Tunisian lines of

Italian San Giogio - AA guardship.

communication. At a meeting at Brenner on June 2 he made his views known to Field-Marshal Keitel. His German colleague was very cool on this question, considering that Cavallero's inclination for strong action would result in the secession of the French Empire, whereas by bargaining with prisoners-of-war and by negotiation, Vichy should be amenable to further concessions. This was also Hitler's view.

Count Ciano met Admiral Darlan at Turin on December 9 and gave no support to the Comando Supremo. Where Darlan brought up the question of the Tunisian ports the Duce's son-in-law cut him short. He wrote. "I interrupted him to say that I had no intention of talking about this subject and had no instructions to do so." There is no satisfactory explanation for Ciano's negative attitude, so clearly prejudicial to the campaign then being fought.

A heavily damaged German tank burns in the desert.

Operation "Crusader"

Sir Claude Auchinleck had organised the troops taking part in "Crusader" into the 8th Army, commanded by Lieutenant-General Sir Alan Cunningham, who had just achieved fame for his lightning defeat of the Italians in Abyssinia. Auchinleck had thus some justification for giving him precedence over his colleague Sir Henry Maitland Wilson, in spite of Churchill's disagreement. He had no idea that Cunningham would not be equal to the strain involved in directing a battle between armoured forces. On the day of the battle the 8th Army was deployed.

This was a completely motorised and partially armoured force, spearheaded by the 7th Armoured Division, which had 469 tanks; this total included 210 Crusaders and 165 American M3 Stuarts.

The British had by no means given up using tanks as infantry support weapons, so the Tobruk garrison and XIII Corps each included an independent brigade equipped with either cruiser or Matilda tanks. In all, 8th Army had 713 gun-armed tanks and could count on over 200 more in reserve to replace any losses.

In the air, Air Vice-Marshal H. Coningham provided the 8th Army with support from the Western Desert Air Force's 16 fighter, eight bomber, and three reconnaissance squadrons. Finally there was Sir Andrew Cunningham, whose fleet's guns were there to give direct support to his brother's operations. This explains the British soldier's characteristically humorous nickname for the operation — "Cunningham, Cunningham, and Coningham".

The Axis deployment might give the impression that Rommel's armour was under the command of General Ettore Bastico and that the "Italian Supreme Commander in North Africa" could control General Gambara's XX Corps. But the impetuous Panzergruppe Afrika commander had no intention whatsoever of respecting this chain of command, and went over Bastico's head to appeal directly to the Comando Supremo, or even to Hitler, when he did not agree with Cavallero's decisions.

Panzergruppe Afrika was formed on August 15 and this enabled Rommel to hand over command of the Afrika Korps to General Cruewell. The 5th Light Division was renamed 21st Panzer Division, but retained its original composition. The Afrika Division comprised only two infantry battalions, recruited from former German volunteers in the French Foreign Legion, to whom Hitler

While the Italian XXI Corps was to overrun Tobruk, the Afrika Korps — some German units and the whole "Savona" Division — would make contact with the British on the Sidi Omar–Capuzzo–Halfaya–Sollum front. Ready for any eventuality, the 15th and 21st Panzer Divisions were stationed in the Gambut area and further south. Finally, Gambara had placed the "Ariete" Armoured Division around the Bir et Gubi watering place and the "Trieste" Motorised Division around Bir Hakeim.

The Axis forces thus amounted to ten divisions, against the 8th Army's six divisions. But it should not be overlooked that the large Italian units were considerably under-strength and that Rommel's supplies of food and fuel were more and more uncertain. As for the armoured forces, General Cunningham had 713 gun-armed tanks, the Italians 146, and the Germans 174.

These are the approximate figures of the forces involved. But when one gets down to brass tacks the British superiority was reduced by certain technical factors. The Matilda had well-known defects and the Crusaders and other cruisers were subject to frequent mechanical faults. In addition the Stuart or M3, driven by an aero engine requiring a high octane fuel, displayed an alarming tendency to catch fire.

But this is not all. Whereas none of the British tanks had weapons more powerful than 40-mm (37-mm for the American M3), half of the Afrika Korps' 139 Pzkw III's were fitted with a 5-cm rather than 3.7-cm gun, and their 35 Pzkw IV's already had a 7.5-cm. Ballistically, the heavier the projectile the more consistent its speed, giving it a longer range and a greater armour-piercing potential. With their 4½-pounder (5-cm) and 15-pounder (7.5-cm) shells, the Germans had an important advantage over their opponents' 40-mm shells, weighing only two pounds.

On the tactical level, it appears that the Germans had struck a better balance between tanks, infantry, and artillery than the 8th Army, and that their radio communications were more reliable. One should also remember Rommel's formidable defensive weapon — the 8.8-cm antiaircraft gun. Used in an anti-tank role, it soon became a decisive factor on the battlefields of the Western Desert. The "88" as it was called by the British was notorious, and assumed the status of an all-purpose wonder weapon, which could destroy any British tank at any range. One British officer, captured and under interrogation, expressed the opinion that it was unfair to use antiaircraft guns against tanks. His captors replied that it was equally unfair for the British to use tanks whose armour nothing but the "88" would penetrate!

Auchinleck perseveres

For Cunningham, in his Maddalena H.Q., the reversals occurring since November 19 were an immense strain, and seemed to offer sufficient justification for an order to retreat. But in the evening of the 23rd, Sir Claude Auchinleck appeared in his mobile caravan H. Q. and ordered him to continue the attack. Auchinleck later wrote: "My opinion was different from Cunningham's. I thought Rommel was probably in as bad shape as we were, especially with Tobruk unvanquished behind him, and I ordered the offensive to continue. I certainly gambled (in fact, by going on we might have lost all) and Cunningham might very well have proved to be right and I wrong!"

At the same moment, his opponent, writing to his wife, claimed to be "well, in excellent spirits and full of confidence." In spite of this, Rommel's raid in the British rear did not succeed in upsetting Auchinleck. "He is making a desperate effort but he won't get very far," he said to Cunningham on November 24. At the end of his order of the day to his troops he told them:

"His position is desperate, and he is trying by lashing out in all directions to distract us from our object, which is to destroy him utterly. We will NOT be distracted and he WILL be destroyed. You have got your teeth into him. Hang on and bite deeper and deeper and hang on till he is finished. Give him NO rest. The general situation in NORTH AFRICA is EXCELLENT. There is only one order: ATTACK AND PURSUE. ALL OUT EVERYONE."

But as he suspected that Cunningham was in no condition to carry out this aggressive plan, he replaced him, on November 26,

44 gallon barrels of fresh water, part of total of 33,000, unloaded from LCT after being bought from Alexandria.

by his own Deputy Chief-of-Staff, Major-General Neil Methuen Ritchie. The former chief of Intelligence in the Panzergruppe Afrika, in his book Panzer Battles, said of this action by Auchinleck at this most critical moment: "This was certainly one of the most important decisions of the war. Auchinleck's will to attack and his strategy of penetration saved 'Crusader' and much else besides." This is a sound judgement.

Although Ritchie took over from Cunningham it was Auchinleck who directed the battle.

On November 25 Scobie received a telegram informing him that the New Zealand Division would attempt to take Sidi Rezegh the next day. The garrison was then expected to occupy El Duda. Scobie launched a new attack on the morning of November 26. After a fierce struggle his infantry overcame the final centre of resistance called "Wolf". But there was still no sign of the arrival of the New Zealanders. At 1300 hours the garrison saw tanks on the horizon, and from one of their turrets three red rockets soared into the blue sky.

The troops cheered wildly, for it was the recognition signal of the 8th Army. Reinforcements were at last in sight!

Fleet Air Arm loading bombs at dessert airfield.

Rommel decides to retreat

Writing to his wife on their silver anniversary, Rommel described his action behind the British lines as a "magnificent success" calling for a "special communiqué" from O.K.W. But he was undoubtedly alone in this view. For not only had he not overcome the 4th Indian Division's stubborn resistance or captured the 8th Army's supply dumps, but he had also left the Panzergruppe without orders for four days, unconcerned that a few hours after his reckless departure he had lost his mobile radio, broken down in the desert.

Liddell Hart's description of this incident in his presentation of Rommel's notebooks gives some idea of the life led in the desert by the commanders themselves:

"A wireless signal from Rommel summoned the commander of the Afrika Korps to the Panzer Group's forward H.Q., which was said to be located near Gambut. After searching for a long time in the darkness they finally discovered a British lorry, which General Cruewell's command car approached with great caution. Inside it, to his good fortune, were no British troops, but Rommel and his Chief-of-Staff, both of whom were unshaven, worn with lack of sleep and caked with dust. In the lorry was a heap of straw as a bed, a can of stale water to drink and a few tins of food. Close by were two wireless trucks and a few dispatch riders. Rommel now gave his instructions for next day's operations."

Meanwhile, XIII Corps had succeeded where XXX Corps had failed. The New Zealand Division, moving through Belhamed, had made contact with the Tobruk garrison, which itself had broken out at El Duda.

With the situation becoming more critical, Lieutenant-Colonel Westphal took it upon himself to pass over the head of his untraceable chief and recall to the Tobruk sector the 21st Panzer Division, which was unattached south of Sollum. When he returned to his H. Q. on November 27, Rommel tacitly endorsed this initiative and without any pause mounted a new operation designed to bring him victory. Some very confused engagements followed, during which the New Zealand Division was cut in two and part of it thrown back to Tobruk. The Germans were becoming exhausted, however, and the 21st Panzer Division's commander, General von Ravenstein, was captured in the confusion.

Auchinleck's reinforcement of the 8th Army had been timely, and the rapidly reorganised XXX Corps again made its presence felt in the battle. Rommel, on the other hand, had to rely on a mere handful of tanks in the decisive days that lay ahead. He had been warned that no supplies of any consequence could be delivered before the latter half of December. So on December 5 he withdrew his forces attacking east of Tobruk, and the next day, after a counter-attack had failed, gave the order for a general retreat. He left to the "Savona" Division the honour of holding out as long as possible in the Bardia–Sollum–Halfaya area.

The British enter Benghazi

Whatever judgement one makes about Rommel's methods, the basic soundness of his decision must be admitted. Moreover he conducted the retreat in a masterly fashion, dealing sharp blows to the British whenever they became too hurried in pursuit. On Christmas Day, General Ritchie's advance guard entered Benghazi. But as the year ended, the 8th Army had not succeeded in intercepting

Rommel, although desert patrols had occupied the Jalo oasis. He was now securely in position behind the El Agheila–Marada strongpoint, leaving behind him 340 tanks destroyed since November 18. On January 17 the "Savona" Division, its food and ammunition exhausted, surrendered to General Villiers, commander of the 2nd South African Division, which had relieved the 4th Indian Division. 32,000 prisoners, 9,000 of them Germans, were taken by the 8th Army in two months. The 8th Army itself had lost 18,000 in killed, wounded and prisoners.

In Washington, Churchill was jubilant over this limited, but undeniable, victory. In a few weeks' time, he thought, Auchinleck would begin Operation "Acrobat", which would complete the destruction of the Axis forces in North Africa and take Ritchie from El Agheila to the Tunisian frontier. Then, under the agreement just reached with President Roosevelt, Operation "Gymnast" would be launched. With or without the consent of the Vichy Government, an Anglo-American expeditionary force would invade Morocco and Algeria.

Enter Kesselring

Hitler's assistance to his ally did not stop there. With the Italians' agreement he signed Directive No. 38 on December 2, ordering a unified command of the Axis forces in the central Mediterranean under a Supreme Commander "South"

(Oberbefehlshaber Süd).

This was Field-Marshal Kesselring, commander of Luftflotte II. He was given a three-fold task:

"To win mastery of the air and sea in the area between Southern Italy and North Africa in order to ensure communications with Libya and Cyrenaica, and particularly to neutralise Malta. Secondly, to co-operate with the German and allied forces operating in North Africa. Thirdly, to paralyse enemy movements in the Mediterranean, including supplies to Tobruk and Malta, working in close co-operation with the available German and Italian naval forces."

Kesselring took command of the Luftwaffe air and anti-aircraft units already in the Mediterranean, and was reinforced by II Fliegerkorps (General Loerzer), withdrawn from the Eastern Front. So the Soviet allies obtained some benefit from British strategy between Malta and Suez.

But these were only half measures by Hitler, for the Supreme Commander "South", or O.B.S. as he was abbreviated, was nowhere in the same class as Eisenhower, Nimitz, or MacArthur when it came to commanding a whole theatre of war. In fact, Panzergruppe Afrika refused to acknowledge his supreme authority, thus very likely prejudicing the outcome of Axis operations. It remained to be proved that this Bavarian, a former artilleryman turned pilot, had a better overall conception of modern combined operations than the Württemberger, a former mountain infantryman converted to tanks. In addition, subordinate to the Comando Supremo, O.K.W., and even Reichsmarschall Göring, Kesselring's position was a most ambiguous one. In spite of all this, he was still able to redress the balance in the central Mediterranean for a time.

The naval balance begins to swing

During the night of December 18 and 19, Force K was pursuing an Italian convoy heading for North Africa when it ran into a minefield. Neptune struck four mines in succession and sank with all her crew except one leading seaman. Aurora and Penelope survived, but were so badly damaged that they remained unseaworthy for many long weeks. The destroyer Kandahar made a courageous attempt to help Neptune but her stern was blown off by another mine and she sank on the spot.

Italian human torpedoes

Also on December 18, at 2100 hours, with admirable precision, the Italian submarine Sciré (Lieutenant Valerio Borghese) managed to launch three manned torpedoes less than one and a half miles from the lighthouse overlooking Alexandria's main channel. Seated astride their machines, in pairs, the six daring men slipped in behind a returning group of destroyers and aimed for their allotted targets: De la Penne and Bianchi for Valiant, Marceglia and Schergat for Queen Elizabeth, and Martellota and Marino for the large tanker Sagona. Once under the hulls of their targets, they removed the explosive warheads of their torpedoes, suspended them from the bottom of the vessels and set the detonators. All this was done in pitch darkness over 30 feet below the surface.

Sagona blew up first, at dawn on December 20. Then came

Valiant, with De la Penne and Bianchi aboard. They had been picked up during the night but had uttered no word about their mission, of which they might have been the first victims. At about 0625 hours, Admiral Cunningham was on the rear deck of Queen Elizabeth inspecting the damage to Valiant when the explosion from Marceglia and Schergat's torpedo flung him four or five feet in the air.

As Roskill points out, "both battleships were seriously flooded and incapacitated for many months. Fortunately it was possible to keep them on even keels and the enemy's … air reconnaissance failed to reveal the full measure of success achieved." But it would be months before they rejoined the fleet, and meanwhile, apart from destroyers Cunningham had no more than four light cruisers under his command, including the old antiaircraft cruiser Carlisle. The Italian Navy, thanks to its mines and midget submarines, had gained, in a single night, a considerable advantage in the Mediterranean. It is true, however, that it did not have enough supplies of oil fuel to make use of this advantage, and so the situation continued to deteriorate in 1942.

Crisis point for Allied seapower

Taking a general view of all the theatres of operations, it can be concluded that between November 25 and December 20, 1941, the Anglo-American forces had lost five of their 33 major vessels, and eight others were out of commission for some months. It may be argued that aircraft-carriers were taking the place of battleships. This is no doubt true, but Japan led the field in this category, with ten to her nearest rival's eight.

German radio station near Tobruk.

Rommel observes retreal of Allies.

British strategy in the Middle East most disastrously reflected the increasing menace of events in the Far East.

We have seen how, when it reached the Cape, the 18th Division, originally intended for General Auchinleck, was redirected to Singapore, where it arrived just in time to be swallowed up in the capitulation of February 15. The 5th Division was also diverted from the Eastern Mediterranean theatre and split up into brigades, some to be used against Diego-Suarez (Operation "Ironclad") and others in Burma.

In addition to these failed expectations, G.H.Q. Cairo also had taken away from it, on orders from London, 150 tanks and three divisions: the 70th, which had defended Tobruk and was sent to

Ceylon, and the 6th and 7th Australian which, as we have seen, were sent home at the urgent request of Prime Minister Curtin.

Far from receiving the reinforcements he thought he could count on, Air Chief-Marshal Tedder, Air Officer Commanding Middle East, had to lose four fighter squadrons. Finally, owing to the Japanese threat to the Indian Ocean, the Admiralty was quite unable to repair the terrible damage caused to the Mediterranean Fleet. Sir Andrew Cunningham had therefore to do as best he could without battleships, aircraft-carriers, and heavy cruisers.

As far as concerns the forces which Sir Arthur Tedder deployed with such skill, their failed expectations arose not only from the fact that new theatres of operations in the Far East were being equipped with formations due to them on the eve of Pearl Harbor, but also because hundreds of fighters and light bombers for the R.A.F. were sent to Murmansk and Archangel, and U.S. military aid to Russia meant that the delivery of planes to Great Britain had had to be slowed down.

But for all that and in accordance with the decisions taken at the "Arcadia" Conference, Auchinleck was still required to mount Operation "Acrobat", which was to take the 8th Army from Agedabia to the Tunisian frontier. Naturally he argued that for the moment, his supply difficulties and the depletion of his forces ruled out any early renewed offensive. The forward troops of the 8th Army were in positions hardly suited to even a defensive action, but G.H.Q. Cairo did not consider the enemy strong enough for an early counter-offensive.

Rommel's surprise attack

The last days of 1941 had seen a complete reversal of the situation in the Central Mediterranean: the destruction of Force K, based on Malta, the battering of the island-fortress by the concentrated efforts of the Italian Air Force and II and X Fliegerkorps of the Luftwaffe, the weakening of the Mediterranean Fleet-all this had reopened the route to Tripoli to the Axis convoys. Whereas in December, taking into account losses of 19 per cent, only 39,902 tons of war matériel and fuel had been landed, in January 100 per cent of all replacements and supplies loaded in Italy got through to Africa. These amounted to 43,328 tons of matériel and 22,842 tons of liquid fuel. On January 5 one convoy brought in for the Afrika Korps 54 Pzkw III and IV tanks, 20 armoured cars, and some self-propelled guns, Russian

76.2-mm guns on Czech tank chassis, all complete with their crews. For its part, the Italian Mobile Corps, now under the command of General Zingales, got two groups of semoventi, Italian-made 75-mm self-propelled guns which proved very effective. Altogether the Axis armoured strength taken by Rommel out of the El Agheila-Marada line, which was henceforth held by only the Italian XXI and X Corps, was 84 German medium and heavy tanks and 89 Italian medium tanks on January 11, 1942. A further 28 German tanks, newly arrived at Tripoli, were expected to join him soon.

Rommel therefore decided to counterattack, taking advantage immediately of his enemy's scattered forces and hoping thus to catch him by surprise, thin on the ground. He issued the following order of the day to his troops:

"German and Italian soldiers:

"You have already endured hard battles against an enemy vastly superior in numbers to yourselves. Your fighting spirit has not been daunted. We now have material superiority over the enemy in front of us. The army will go over to the attack today to wipe him out.

"I expect every man to give of his best in these decisive days. Long live Italy! Long live Greater Germany! Long live their leaders!"

Surprise was complete, not only at the front for the British XIII Corps but also for G.H.Q. at Cairo. On the Axis side, however, Rommel's move came as a shock for General Bastico and at Rome both for the Comando Supremo and for Field-Marshal Kesselring. In the entry in his diary for January 21 Rommel

German troops advance.

explains his silence in terms which give cause for reflection:

"I had maintained secrecy over the Panzer Group's forthcoming attack eastwards from Marsa Brega and informed neither the Italian nor the German High Command. We knew from experience that Italian Headquarters cannot keep things to themselves and that everything they wireless to Rome gets round to British ears. However, I had arranged with the Quartermaster for the Panzergruppe's order to be posted up in every Cantoniera (Road Maintenance Depot) in Tripolitania on the 21st January — the day the attack was due to take place."

Without expressing an opinion of the danger of the leaks in Rome which he feared, and which in his view entitled him to

deploy the Italian troops under him without reference to General Bastico, we would observe that he did not need to fear such leaks at O.K.W. If Rommel kept his intentions secret from his superiors it was because he feared they would forbid him from carrying them out.

The Benghazi road cut

In the first part of this battle Rommel found himself facing the British 1st Armoured Division. Newly arrived in Africa, it had only 150 tanks, and had been split into three groups which could not be self-supporting. The same dispersion was evident at the next level upwards, XIII Corps: the 4th Indian Division which, for logistic reasons, had got no further forward than Benghazi,

Tobruk - knocked out British tanks after last breakout attempt.

could not help the 1st Armoured, and the latter was even less likely to get help from the 7th Armoured Division, which had been sent back to Tobruk to be brought up to strength.

Moving forward along two axes of attack with five armoured and motorised divisions, the Italian Mobile Corps along the Via Balbia and the Afrika Korps further inland, Rommel had no difficulty in sweeping before him the 22nd Guards Brigade and, in the evening of January 22, he camped at Agedabia, having advanced 56 miles in 48 hours. In particular he had cut the road to Benghazi, to the surprise and dismay of his enemy. The following day he set about the destruction of the opposing forces by an encircling movement. Whilst General Zingales engaged the bulk of the 1st Armoured Division in the west, he drove the Afrika Korps north-east towards Antelat then turned south-east, and due south from Saunnu. How ever, in its haste to close the trap round the enemy, his vanguard left Saunnu before the head of the 15th Panzer Division reached it and the British escaped through the gap, though in a bad state and leaving a great deal of matériel behind.

Hawker Hurricane stands ready on a Malta airfield.

The successes of the Axis forces in Cyrenaica resounded like a thunderclap on the banks of the Thames. On January 25, the Prime Minister, "much disturbed" by the report that the 8th Army was intending to evacuate Benghazi and Derna, cabled General Auchinleck:

"It seems to me this is a serious crisis, and one to me quite unexpected. Why should they all be off so quickly? Why should the 4th (British-) Indian Division not hold out at Benghazi, like the Huns at Halfaya? The kind of retirement now evidently envisaged by subordinate officers implies the failure of 'Crusader' and the ruin of 'Acrobat'." In his memoirs, Churchill says that he refused to accept General Auchinleck's explanation that the

"only" reason for this defeat, which was "so serious and heavy with consequences", had been the mechanical unreliability of the British armour about which Auchinleck had complained previously. Churchill's anger is understandable, but no one could deny that this very real inferiority of the British tanks compared with the Panzers weighed heavily in the balance. But again, what so irritated the Prime Minister in the event was not only that "Acrobat" (the advance on Tripoli) had to be postponed, but that there was also now the greater danger to Malta after the 8th Army's retreat to the Gazala–Bir Hakeim line, and this at a time when the Luftwaffe's II and X Fliegerkorps and the Italian Air Force were pounding the island.

From the airstrips in the Benghazi area, some 420 miles from

Malta convoy - aerial view of some of the escorting warships, including cruisers and aircraft carriers.

Valletta, or, at a pinch, from Derna (530 miles), the R.A.F. could give continuous support to convoys from Alexandria supplying the beleaguered island. This was impossible from Tobruk (580 miles) and, to make matters worse, the "bump" of Cyrenaica, retaken by Rommel, was only 190 miles from Crete. The seas between were thus at the mercy of Axis cross-fire. Nevertheless, in January Admiral Cunningham succeeded in getting through to Malta three merchant ships and the supply-ship Breconshire for the loss of only one vessel. But February's convoy was a total failure: out of three merchant ships which left Alexandria, one had

to be sent in to Tobruk because of the damage caused by enemy bombs, a second was sunk, and the third had to be scuttled.

The second battle of Sirte

Admiral Cunningham could not abandon Malta to her dire fate. He therefore organised another convoy of three merchant ships and the supply-ship Breconshire, which had meanwhile returned from Valletta. Rear-Admiral Philip Vian, of Altmark fame, who had commanded the previous convoys, was put in charge of this risky operation and, on March 20 he set sail from Alexandria with an escort of four light cruisers, ten destroyers,

Air raid on Malta. Smoke and dust rising from German attack.

Italians would not join battle, but preferred to await the arrival of the battleship Littorio, which appeared on the scene towards 1640 hours.

Admiral Iachino's plan was to get between Malta and the convoy and then wipe out the ships, but the sirocco, blowing in gusts from the south-east, allowed Vian to take cover behind a smoke-screen, which the Italians, having no radar, could not penetrate. When one of the British cruisers did appear out of the smoke, the enemy could not engage it because of the spray and the smoke which obscured their range-finders. Thus the Italians' enormous superiority in firepower was of little avail to them. At nightfall Iachino made a last attempt to get near to the convoy but he had to withdraw, driven off by the volleys of torpedoes fired off at him by the British destroyers as they counter-attacked and, as none of his ships was equipped for night-fighting, he had to abandon the action a little before 1900 hours.

The result of this second battle of Sirte was not as disappointing for the Italians as it might at first have seemed. Admiral Cunningham had lost the destroyers Havock and Kingston, which had been heavily damaged and had had to make for Malta. The convoy, having had to sail south-west for hours, could not now reach Valletta before dawn on the 23rd. This caused the loss by bombing of the Breconshire and one merchant ship: the two survivors reached harbour but were sunk as they were unloading. And so, out of the 26,000 tons of supplies which had left Alexandria only 5,000 reached their destination. On the other hand two Italian destroyers, ploughing on through the storm, sank with most of their crews. The light cruiser Bande

and six Hunt-class destroyer escorts. At dawn on the 22nd he was joined by the cruiser Penelope and the destroyer Legion which had come out from Malta to bring the merchant ships in. But Vian's movements had been spotted off Derna by the Italian submarine Platino and at midnight on the 21st the battleship Littorio, flying the flag of Admiral Iachino, sailed from Taranto, whilst an hour later the cruisers Gorizia, Trento, and Bande Nere left Messina. Each of these two detachments was escorted by four destroyers. At 1427 hours Rear-Admiral Parona's three cruisers made contact with the enemy, whereupon Vian made his convoy turn south-west, covered by the guns of the anti-aircraft cruiser Carlisle and the Hunts, and engaged the Italians with the rest of his forces. The

Nere was so severely damaged in the same storm that she had to be sent to La Spezia for repairs. On the way there she was sunk by the submarine Urge (Lieutenant-Commander E. P. Tomkinson). This was a compensation for the loss of the light cruiser Naiad, which had gone down under Rear-Admiral Vian on February 11 in the previous year, torpedoed off the coast of Egypt by U-565.

The tragic situation of Malta

The bombardment of Malta, which had been intensified from mid-December 1941 to the end of February, became in March a veritable ordeal by fire: in 31 days 4,927 bombing sorties were flown against the island, and in April no fewer than 9,599 dropped 6,700 tons of bombs. In the Grand Harbour three destroyers, including Kingston were sunk and the valiant Penelope was so riddled with shrapnel that her crew facetiously renamed her Pepperpot. To avoid destruction, the submarines of the 10th Flotilla had to submerge by day with reduced crews.

For its part, the island's air force was decimated in battles in the air or wiped out on the ground. On January 31 there were only 28 fighters left; a fortnight later, there were only 11. In this almost desperate situation help came from the west, that is from Force H, now commanded by Rear-Admiral E. N. Syfret who had taken over from Sir James Somerville. On March 6 the old Argus, the first "flat-top" of any navy in the world, and the Eagle sent 15 Spitfires, more capable than the Hurricanes of dealing with the Messerschmitt Bf 109F's of X Fliegerkorps. This operation was successfully repeated on March 21 and 29.

Generous gesture by America

To speed up the reinforcement of Malta's defence, Winston Churchill appealed to President Roosevelt. On April 1, after describing the tragic situation of Malta's defenders, who had only 20 to 30 fighters as against the 600 of the Axis, and the difficulties of sending them enough Spitfires on the carriers at his disposal, he added:

"Would you be willing to allow your carrier Wasp to do one of these trips provided details are satisfactorily agreed between the Naval Staffs? With her broad lifts, capacity and length, we estimate that Wasp could take 50 or more Spitfires. Unless it were necessary for her to fuel, Wasp could proceed through the Straits

British tanker about to sink after German aerial bombing.

Luftwaffe - Junkers, the pilot burning with the wreckage.

at night without calling at Gibraltar until on the return journey, as the Spitfires would be embarked in the Clyde. Thus, instead of not being able to give Malta any further Spitfires during April, a powerful Spitfire force could be flown into Malta at a stroke and give us a chance of inflicting a very severe and possibly decisive check on the enemy. Operation might take place during third week of April."

President Roosevelt responded to his ally's request in a fine spirit of comradeship. Thus on April 20 Wasp, which had got within 620 miles of Malta, sent off 47 Spitfires; these were reduced to six four days later after redoubled attacks by the Luftwaffe. Churchill had therefore to ask for a second run by the

American aircraft-carrier and he did this with an argument worth mentioning. He cabled the President on April 20:

"Without this aid I fear Malta will be pounded to bits. Meanwhile its defence is wearing out the enemy's Air Force and effectively aiding Russia."

Roosevelt responded again with help and Wasp went back into the Mediterranean on May 9. Together with Eagle she sent off 64 Spitfires to Malta; these were followed by a further 17 on May 18 from the British carrier alone. Churchill relates in his memoirs:

"It may be well here to complete the story of the Wasp. On May 9 she successfully delivered another important flight of Spitfires to struggling Malta. I made her a signal: 'Who said a wasp couldn't sting twice?' The Wasp thanked me for my 'gracious' message. Alas, poor Wasp! She left the dangerous Mediterranean for the Pacific and on September 15 was sunk by Japanese torpedoes. Happily her gallant crew were saved. They had been a link in our chain of causation."

The fact remains, however, that the population and the garrison of the island-fortress were put on short rations and that their supply of flour was due to run out on about June 15.

Axis plans against Malta

For a long time now Grand-Admiral Raeder had been maintaining to the Führer that the war would be won at Suez and Basra, but that the capture of these two objectives depended on the seizure of Malta. The day after Admiral Ciliax had forced a passage through the Straits of Dover, Hitler was somewhat more receptive to these ideas and, at the end of February, Field-Marshal

Kesselring could write to Marshal Cavallero without fear of repudiation:

"The Führer is in complete agreement with the Italian Command for definite action against the island of Malta. He is following the development of this action with great interest; he will give it all possible support unless Britain attempts a landing on such a scale that it would require a maximum concentration of our forces."

And a few days later, Keitel, the Chief-of-Staff of O.K.W., wrote along the same lines to his Italian opposite number, who welcomed the news as he had long been in favour of this operation, which he considered risky but necessary. Hence on April 12 a Planning H. Q. was set up under General Fassi. The two dictators met on April 30 at Klessheim near Salzburg, and Cavallero, warmly supported by Kesselring, put forward his plan. This produced no practical or theoretical objections, Hitler merely remarking that "an operation like this must be planned down to the smallest detail for if it fails there can be no going back to the beginning." On this agreement and the promise of substantial German support, the Chief-of-Staff of the Comando Supremo drew up his plan for a simultaneous attack on the islands of Malta and Gozo.

The operation was called "Herkules" by the Germans. They also contributed a number of heavy tanks and some 300 transport aircraft. The axis powers would thus have eight divisions against the Allies' garrison on the two islands of 30,000–35,000 men under Lieutenant-General Sir William Dobbie.

It had been originally planned that the assault on Malta

should precede Rommel's offensive. This was to start from the line Sollum–Halfaya–Sidi Omar. The need to train the "Folgore" Division paratroopers, however, compelled Cavallero to reverse this order of priority and the resultant delay was to have incalculable consequences.

Takali Aerodrome bomb craters.

RAF pilot and Supermarine Spitfire.

It was on the afternoon of June 21, in the elegant White House study of President Roosevelt, that Winston Churchill first learnt of the fall of Tobruk. According to Churchill's memoirs, on learning of the catastrophe, the President dropped everything and immediately summoned General Marshall. Lord Alanbrooke, on the other hand, in the 1946 additions to his war diaries, would have us believe that it was General Marshall himself who delivered the bad news to the two statesmen, as they conferred in the Oval Room of the White House.

"I can remember this incident as if it had occurred yesterday. Churchill and I were standing beside the President's desk talking to him, when Marshall walked in with a pink piece of paper containing a message of the fall of Tobruk. Neither Winston nor I had contemplated such an eventuality and it was a staggering blow. I cannot remember what the actual words were that the President used to convey his sympathy, but I remember vividly being impressed by the tact and real heartfelt sympathy which lay behind these words. There was not one word too much nor one word too little."

"Second Front Now"

Eisenhower believed that there would need to be definite signs of cracking German morale before an attack on the fortified coast of Western Europe could be attempted. "This was a very definite conviction, held by some of our experienced soldiers, sailors, and airmen, that the fortified coast of western Europe could not be successfully attacked. Already much was known of the tremendous effort the German was making to insure the integrity of his Atlantic Wall." Although American military opinion favoured a landing in 1942, the British, partly influenced by their experiences against Turkish batteries in the Dardanelles; were convinced this would not be practicable before 1943.

Hitler was nevertheless worried about the possibility of a cross-channel attack. His directive of July 9 to Army, Navy and Air Force included the following assessment: "Our swift and massive victories may force Great Britain to choose between launching a large-scale invasion, with a view to opening a second front, or seeing Russia eliminated as a military and political factor. Hence it is highly probable that we shall soon face an enemy landing within the O.K.H. command area."

Operation "Gymnast", a landing in French North Africa under American command, was, despite initial American scepticism, seen as the only viable alternative to an attack on the French coast, and it was re-christened Operation "Torch".

But Roosevelt did not stop at mere eloquent expressions of sympathy; quite spontaneously, he immediately asked what he could do to temper the effects of the disaster inflicted upon the British Army. His first idea was to send out the American 1st Armoured Division to the Middle East, but the carrying out of such a project would have created enormous difficulties; he and General Marshall, therefore, in a spirit of comradeship rarely known in coalitions, offered to refit the 8th Army, by giving it the 300 Sherman tanks that had just been distributed to the American armoured units. To complete this most generous gift, 100 self-propelled 105-mm guns were also offered. But even that was not all, for when the cargo vessel carrying the 300 tank engines was torpedoed and sunk off Bermuda, "without a single word from us the President and Marshall put a further supply of engines into another fast ship and dispatched it to overtake the convoy. 'A friend in need is a friend indeed.'"

The entry into active service of the 31-ton M4 Sherman tank upgraded the hitting power of the 8th Army in the Battle of El Alamein. Its long-barrelled (37.5 calibre) 75-mm gun was almost as good as the shorter (24 calibre) 7.5-cm gun generally fitted to the heaviest tanks (the Pzkw IV) of the Panzerarmee Afrika; secondly it had a less obtrusive shape than its predecessor, the M3 Grant; finally, the latter's awkward sponson was replaced in the Sherman tank by a turret capable of traversing through 360 degrees.

For diplomatic reasons it was not revealed at the time that the Sherman was what General Sir Brian Horrocks, commander of XIII Corps at El Alamein, later in his memoirs called "a brilliant example of Anglo-American co-operation". American engineers were in charge of the tank's mechanical features (engine, transmission, and tracks), whilst the armament derived from researches carried out by a British team. It was, apparently, because he wanted the aid the Americans were so generously giving to receive full public recognition, that Churchill suppressed the extent of British participation.

R.A.F. reinforcements

At the same time (summer 1942), the Italo-German air forces fighting in North Africa finally lost their last remnants of superiority over the R.A.F., now being regularly reinforced by deliveries of American and British aircraft, which, technically and tactically, were of the highest quality: there was, for example, the Supermarine Spitfire Mark V interceptor and the Hawker Hurricane III) fighter-bomber, nicknamed the "tin-opener", because its 40-mm armour-piercing shells tore through the thickest Panzer armour with considerable ease. Later came the excellent North American P-51 Mustang fighter capable of 390 mph, and with a ceiling of 31,000 feet. Roosevelt's sympathetic understanding of Britain's needs also made it possible to increase to 117 the number of strategic bombers posted to this theatre, when the four-engined American Consolidated B-24 Liberator bomber joined the British-built Handley-Page Halifax.

It therefore follows that the R.A.F. not only recovered, conclusively and permanently, mastery of the air, but also that it was able to give the 8th Army, in both its defensive and offensive rôles, support that daily became more powerful and better organised. In his book on the war in the air, Air Vice-Marshal J. E. Johnson has traced this development very precisely: "Slowly, by trial, error, and the foresight of gifted men, not only airmen, the pattern of air support for the soldiers again took shape. Fighters to grind down the enemy bomber and fighter forces; fighters which could then be armed with bombs to attack the enemy ground forces; fighters which, armed or not with bombs, were always capable of protecting themselves and providing protection for the bombers. A bomber force which was as capable of bombing enemy airfields and installations as of attacking troops on the ground. A reconnaissance force to be the eyes of both Army and Air Force Commanders."

Among the "gifted men" whom the author mentions, pride of place must go to General Bernard Law Montgomery, who on taking over command of the 8th Army, set up his H.Q. next to that of Air Vice-Marshal Coningham, commanding the Desert Air Force, as the Middle East's tactical air force was called.

Alexander takes over from Auchinleck

At all events, the C.I.G.S., General Brooke, went to Cairo, inspecting Gibraltar and Malta on the way-but not alone, as he would have liked; Churchill had also decided to go out and see for himself what the situation was like, and had summoned General Wavell, C.-in-C. India, and Field-Marshal Smuts, both men whose opinion he valued, to meet him in Cairo.

"Had General Auchinleck or his staff lost the confidence of the Desert Army? If so, should he be relieved, and who could succeed him?" According to his memoirs, these were the two big questions that brought Churchill to Cairo, where he landed on the morning of August 4, only a few minutes before the C.I.G.S. In reality his mind was already made up, as is proved by the fact that on August 6, at dawn, he went to see Brooke, just as the latter was

Sir Claude John Eyre Auchinleck North Africa 23rd July 1942.

getting up ("practically naked"), and told him that he had decided to split the Middle East theatre into two. Relegated to Basra or Baghdad, Auchinleck would be given the new Persia and Iraq Command, separated from the rest of Middle East Command, which Churchill now offered to Brooke. The latter asked not to be appointed on the grounds that this was no time to disorganise the Imperial General Staff, and that in any case he had no knowledge of desert warfare. But that evening he confided to his diary:

"Another point which I did not mention was that, after working with the P.M. for close on nine months, I do feel at last that I can exercise a limited amount of control on some of his activities and that at last he is beginning to take my advice. I feel, therefore, that, tempting as the offer is, by accepting it I should definitely be taking a course which would on the whole help the war least. Finally, I could not bear the thought that Auchinleck might think that I had come out here on purpose to work myself into his shoes."

General Sir Harold Alexander was born in 1891 and entered the British Army by means of Sandhurst. He served with great distinction with the Irish Guards in World War I and after the war in the Baltic States and in India. Alexander commanded the British rearguard at Dunkirk very ably, and further enhanced his reputation as G.O.C. Southern Command in 1940 and by his masterly retreat through Burma in 1942. He was then appointed Eisenhower's deputy for Operation "Torch", but was almost immediately asked to take over from Auchinleck in the Western Desert. With Montgomery commanding in the field, and Alexander in overall command, Rommel was pushed steadily back out of Egypt and Libya into Tunisia. February 1942 saw Alexander's appointment as Deputy Supreme Commander in North Africa and commander of the 18th Army Group. By May the Axis forces in Africa had been destroyed, and Alexander started planning the invasion of Italy.

The new team

Brooke having thus refused, for the most honourable of reasons, Sir Harold Alexander was asked that very evening, on Brooke's recommendation, to take over the Middle East Command. A happy choice, for the new commander had shown the same imperturbability and resourcefulness at Dunkirk as later in the Burma jungle, and, in addition, wore his authority easily. "Calm, confident and charming as always" was the impression the difficult Montgomery received on their first meeting at G.H.Q. Cairo. Alexander had just been appointed deputy to General Eisenhower, as commander of the British 1st Army taking part in "Torch", and Eisenhower now had to be asked to release him for this new post.

Originally, and in spite of Brooke's opposition, General W. H. E. Gott had been appointed to command the 8th Army, but the aircraft in which he was travelling was forced down by two German fighters; whilst he was helping other passengers caught in the wreckage, a second attack caused the plane to explode, leaving no survivors, and his successor, Brooke's candidate, took over and was told to get out to Cairo immediately. This was Lieutenant-General Bernard L. Montgomery -who had just introduced himself to Eisenhower as Alexander's successor as commander of the 1st Army. Small wonder that on being deprived of his second deputy in 48 hours, Eisenhower cynically asked, "Are the British taking 'Torch' seriously?"

To replace General Corbett, Alexander chose as his chief-of-staff Lieutenant-General R. McCreery; he was very popular, and Alexander wrote of him that "he was one of those officers who is as successful at H.Q. as at the head of his troops" and "faithful friend and companion" to him personally. Thus was formed the brilliant team which, with Air Chief Marshal Sir Arthur Tedder and Admiral Sir Henry Harwood, led the 8th Army from El Alamein to Tripoli in less than nine months.

General Auchinleck, relieved of his command because he had refused to attack before mid-September, accepted his disgrace with dignity, but refused the consolation prize that Churchill offered.

Churchill's instructions

On August 10 the British Prime Minister, accompanied by Generals Wavell and Brooke, flew to Moscow to inform the Russians of the Anglo-American decision to abandon Operation "Sledgehammer" in favour of Operation "Torch". But before leaving Cairo, Churchill had sent Alexander hand-written instructions, fixing his tasks in the following manner:

"1. Your prime and main duty will be to take or destroy at the earliest opportunity the German-Italian Army commanded by Field-Marshal Rommel together with all its supplies and establishments in Egypt and Libya.

2. You will discharge or cause to be discharged such other duties as pertain to your command without prejudice to the task

described in paragraph 1, which must be considered paramount in His Majesty's interests."

Operation "Pedestal"

Whilst Churchill and his advisers were setting off for Moscow via Teheran, 14 merchant ships slipped through the Straits of Gibraltar under cover of dense fog. The interruption of convoys to Archangel had allowed the Admiralty to devote considerable resources to this new operation of supplying Malta: three aircraft-carriers, Eagle, Victorious, and Indomitable with their 72 fighters; the two battleships Nelson and Rodney; seven cruisers, one of which was an anti-aircraft vessel; 24 destroyers; two tankers; four corvettes; and eight submarines. In addition, the old aircraft carrier Furious, with an escort of eight destroyers, was able to fly off 38 Spitfires to Malta. The convoy had 14 merchantmen.

This considerable naval force was under the overall command of Vice-Admiral Sir Neville Syfret, commanding Force H. Rear-Admiral H. M. Burrough, with four cruisers and 12 destroyers, was the convoy's immediate escort; bearing in mind what had happened the previous June, he was to escort the convoy as far as Malta. Such were the outlines of "Pedestal".

However, it was all the more difficult to keep such a large-scale undertaking secret as the Italian secret service had paid informers in the Bay of Algeciras, and the Germans and Italians were able to prepare, right down to the smallest details, a plan to intercept and destroy the "Pedestal" convoy. This shows the close co-operation which now existed between Supermarina, under Admiral Arturo Riccardi, Superaero (General Rino Corso Fougier), and the

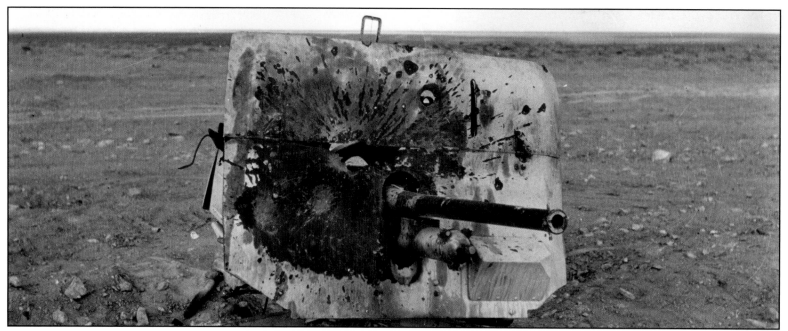

Knocked out British anti tank gun.

Germans, Field-Marshal Kesselring and Admiral Weichold. However, they had to recognise that they would not be able to use the four battleships available to them, so great had the fuel crisis become since June 15. The attack would therefore be carried out by aerial and naval forces.

The Allies suffer

It was Lieutenant Rosenbaum (U-73) who opened the Axis score when, early on the afternoon of August 11, a salvo of four torpedoes struck the aircraft-carrier Eagle, and sank her in eight minutes, thus ending the career of this fine old ship, which had played so vital a part in the supplying of Malta. On the Allies side, a few hours later the destroyer Wolverine rammed and sank the Italian submarine Vagabur as it was trying to torpedo Furious, which, having accomplished her mission, was returning to Gibraltar.

Throughout August 12, the Hurricanes of the three aircraft-carriers repulsed successive attacks from some 200 dive-bombers and torpedo-carrying planes, which had taken off from the Sardinian bases of Elmas and Decimomannu; in conjunction with the anti-aircraft fire of the convoy, the Hurricanes destroyed 28 aircraft, so that during this second phase of the battle, the successes of the Axis air forces were meagre indeed: one cargo ship, damaged by a bomb, lagged behind the convoy and was finished off during the night by a motor torpedo boat, while three German Ju 87's scored hits on the flight deck of Indomitable, whose planes were then taken on board Victorious. The destroyer Foresight, which had received a torpedo hit, was scuttled by her own crew, while the destroyer Ithuriel sank the Italian submarine Cobalto.

At 1900 hours, having reached a point north of Bizerta, Syfret, in accordance with instructions, headed for Gibraltar with his support force, wishing Burrough and his convoy a safe journey, a wish which was never granted, for the third and fourth acts of this aero-naval tragedy firmly established the victory of the Axis forces, and especially the Italian Navy.

The last acts of the tragedy started just after 2000 hours, when, near Cape Bon, the two submarines Axum and Dessié (commanded by Lieutenants Ferrini and Scandola) fired eight torpedoes, five of which struck home, sinking the antiaircraft cruiser Cairo, and causing serious damage to one of the convoy's cargo ships (the tanker Ohio) and the cruiser Nigeria, Admiral Burrough's flagship. In the ensuing confusion a further air attack damaged two more merchant ships, which were sunk in the night by Italian naval forces. In addition, at about 2200 hours, the submarine Alagi (Lieutenant Puccini) damaged the cruiser Kenya and sank yet another cargo ship. In the early hours of the 13th the Italian motor torpedo boats, prowling between Cap Bon and Pantelleria, fell upon the remnants of the convoy and attacked continuously until sunrise, sinking four more merchantmen and the cruiser Manchester.

Italy's last victory

But at the same time an equally fierce battle was being waged within the Axis Supreme Command, between Admirals Riccardi and Weichold on the one hand, and Field-Marshal Kesselring and General Fougier on the other; the question at issue was the following: on August 13, should the fighter cover be given to the two squadrons of cruisers charged with finishing off the convoy south of Pantelleria, or should they protect the bomber squadrons, since they would not be able to protect both at the same time?

Unable to decide between the two rival claims, Marshal Cavallero put the question to Mussolini, who decided that the fighters should protect the bombers: a bad decision as the Stuka bombers and torpedo planes sank only one ship, whereas the six cruisers and 11 motor torpedo boats originally due to go into action would almost certainly have finished off the five ships still left of the convoy. To make matters worse, the Italian naval squadron was intercepted on the way back to base by the submarine Unbroken, commanded by Lieutenant Alastair Mars, who scored two direct hits on the Bolzano and the Attendolo, damaging them so badly that they remained out of action till September 1943.

Bragadin's conclusion on this episode is that "the battle of mid-August 1942 marked the swan-song of the Italian Navy, and the last important victory of the Axis in the Mediterranean conflict". How right he was is seen from the fact that of the 85,000 tons of supplies loaded in the Clyde. 53,000 tons went to the bottom but the 32,000 tons that got through to Valletta were sufficient to see the island fortress through till November; and thanks to the admirable devotion to duty of Captain Dudley W. Mason and the crew of Ohio, which in impossible conditions managed to get through 10,000 tons of fuel, the torpedo planes and submarines stationed at Malta were able to engage their offensive against the Italian Navy with renewed vigour, until Rommel was finally and comprehensively defeated.

German tanks in North Africa.

The last Panzer offensive towards Cairo, Alexandria, and the Suez Canal gave rise to two battles. The first was lost by Rommel between August 31 and September 5, 1942; the second, less conclusive, was the verbal battle fought after the war by Churchill and Montgomery on the one hand, and Auchinleck and his chief-of-staff (Major-General Dorman-Smith, who shared his chief's fall from grace in August 1942), on the other. This quarrel has been revived by Correlli Barnett who, in his book The Desert Generals, has passed harsh judgement on both the British Prime Minister and Field-Marshal Montgomery. According to the latter, when he was received at Mena House on August 12, Auchinleck was anything but determined to defend the El Alamein position at all costs if there were an Italo-German offensive. Montgomery writes in his memoirs:

"He asked me if I knew he was to go. I said that I did. He explained to me his plan of operations; this was based on the fact that at all costs the Eighth Army was to be preserved 'in being' and must not be destroyed in battle. If Rommel attacked in strength, as was expected soon, the Eighth Army would fall back on the Delta; if Cairo and the Delta could not be held, the army would retreat southwards up the Nile, and another possibility was a withdrawal to Palestine. Plans were being made to move the Eighth Army H.Q. back up the Nile."

Auchinleck has categorically denied ever having uttered such words to Montgomery, and Montgomery's own publishers later made a disclaimer. Naturally, Auchinleck had considered the possibility of withdrawal. This did not mean, however, that Auchinleck would have deliberately retreated as soon as Rommel had begun his first large-scale manoeuvre, as Montgomery implies. On the contrary, everything seems to indicate that he fully intended to face up to an attack at El Alamein, in accordance with the plans drawn up by Major-General Dorman-Smith. Furthermore, it is fair to ask whether or not the new team at the head of the 8th Army, however determined it might be to fight, would have condemned it to destruction in the event of one of Rommel's typical outflanking movements. In fact, both under Auchinleck and later under Montgomery and Alexander, contingency plans were made to meet the "worst possible case" of a German breakthrough past the Alamein position. The problem of how to cope with such a breakthrough was naturally discussed by the successive sets of command.

Was Dorman-Smith's plan, adopted by Auchinleck, taken over without reference or acknowledgement by Montgomery? This is the claim put forward by Correlli Barnett. In reality, such a plan was forced upon both generals by Rommel's probable tactics, and also by the nature of the terrain, which dominated the surrounding countryside by nearly 200 feet and did not lend itself to the German general's usual outflanking tactics. To this plan, however, Montgomery added personal qualities of dynamism and cunning, which justify him calling the battle his own.

Rommel forced to act precipitately

Faced with an opponent whom he knew to be getting stronger day by day, Rommel realised he had to attack, and quickly, otherwise he would soon be overrun by an opponent superior in numbers and equipment. He had been able to motorise his 90th

Montgomery addresses British and New Zealand armoured troops.

Light Division, and had been reinforced by the 164th Division flown in from the Balkans — but without its vehicles; this was also the case with the parachute troops of the German Ramcke Brigade, and the Italian "Folgore" Division.

In the notes which he has left us, Rommel lays the blame for the failure of his last offensive on the way he was let down by the Comando Supremo, whose head, Marshal Cavallero, never stopped making him the most alluring promises. But it is difficult to accept this criticism, since it was no fault of Cavallero's that Malta was not neutralised and then besieged, instead of the boats of the

British 10th Submarine Flotilla being once more able to use

British Artillery fire on enemy positions in North Africa.

Malta's large harbour from the beginning of July. As a result, Italian supplies lost in transit, about six per cent in July, shot up to 25 per cent of equipment and 41 per cent of fuel in August; indeed, Cavallero's diary for the period reads like an obituary:

"August 25. The Pozarica is torpedoed. August 27. The Camperio is set on fire. August 28. The Dielpi and the Istria are both sunk, the latter with all her crew. August 30. The Sant'Andrea is sunk with 1,300 tons of fuel for the D.A.K."

Another point is that Rommel's criticisms take no account of the fact that his supply lines had become far too long. To get from the front to Benghazi took a week, with a further five days to get to Tripoli for supplies. It is true that Tobruk was better placed,

but it could only take small ships of up to 600 tons, and in any case had suffered very heavy attacks at the hands of the R.A.F. The responsibility for this state of affairs was Rommel's alone since, despite the doubts of Bastico, Cavallero, and Kesselring himself, he had insisted on exploiting his victories by going headlong after the enemy.

The German plan

Rommel's plan of attack included some decoy movements by the Italian X and XXI Corps, reinforced by German elements. These would engage the enemy head-on and prevent him getting wind too soon of the plan of attack. These dummy attacks were to begin at 0200 hours, giving Rommel the whole night to take his armoured forces (consisting of the Italian XX Corps and the Deutsches Afrika Korps) through the left wing of the enemy's lines, and up to 30 miles past their starting point. After this he would regroup his armour and wheel to the north, with the intention of reaching the Alexandria road behind the 8th Army, which would thus be cut off from its communications, caught on the retreat, and annihilated. There would then be a threefold pursuit of the enemy:

1. the Bismarck group (the 21st Panzer Division and the 164th Division) would make for Alexandria;

2. the Afrika Korps (the 15th Panzer Division and the 90th Light Division) would cross the Nile at Cairo and immediately head for the Suez Canal; and

3. the Italian XX Corps (the "Ariete" and "Littorio" Armoured Divisions) and the "Trieste" Motorised Division would clean up any resistance in the Wadi Natrun area.

As Paul Carell has said, this plan had Rommel written all over it. And Colonel Bayerlein, chief-of-staff of the Panzerarmee at this time, has confirmed that it was a tried and tested Rommel tactic, which he had used at Tobruk, Gazala, and Marsa Matrûh. All very true — but the point was that it had been used so often that it was now worn out, and was too typical not to be seen through quite easily. In fact, both the Auchinleck/Dorman-Smith team and General Montgomery made their plans on the assumption that Rommel would do something like this: a deep eastward push into the southern sector of the El Alamein position, followed by a rapid turn up towards the Mediterranean.

When Montgomery assumed command (48 hours earlier than he was supposed to), the 8th Army was deployed as follows:

1. on the right, blocking the way to Alexandria, was Lieutenant-General William H. C. Ramsden's XXX Corps, made up of the 9th Australian, 1st South African, and 5th Indian Divisions; and

2. on the left, Lieutenant-General Brian Horrocks' XIII Corps had the New Zealand Division in the line with the 7th Armoured Division further south, for the purpose of slowing up Rommel's initial push and then making a flank attack as soon as he turned north.

These dispositions did not altogether please Montgomery; he thought in particular that Alam el Halfa ridge was too lightly defended, so he brought in the 44th Division, under Major-General I. T. P. Hughes, and also two armoured brigades of the 10th Armoured Division (a perfect example of the Montgomery "dynamism" mentioned earlier on). All in all, on August 31, the 8th Army had available 712 serviceable tanks, though this figure includes 164 Grants.

In spite of these reinforcements, Montgomery imposed an essentially defensive strategy upon his army. He thought that too often in the past the British tanks had been launched into attacks or counterattacks that Rommel had cunningly channelled so as to bring them up against his redoubtable anti-tank guns. This battle would therefore be essentially an artillery duel, with tank movements restricted to exceptional cases; so his tanks dug in. "Don't let yourself get bitten!" he never tired of repeating to Horrocks, upon whose corps the brunt of the Axis offensive was soon to fall.

Rommel's lack of certainty

To launch his attack Rommel would have liked to take advantage of the full moon of August 26, but the supply difficulties mentioned above led to its postponement until August 30. That evening, just before H-hour, which had been fixed for 2200 hours, a stirring order of the day was read out to the troops, reminding them of their glorious past exploits, and exhorting them to the decisive effort:

"Our army, reinforced by new divisions, is moving in to annihilate the enemy.

"In the course of these decisive days, I expect every man to give of his best.

"Long live Fascist Italy! Long live Germany! Long live our glorious leaders!"

But Rommel was less certain of a successful outcome to the operation than his own proclamation indicated. Writing to his wife a few hours earlier, he had told her, after pointing out the deficiencies that still remained in his army:

"I've taken the risk, for it will be a long time before we get such favourable conditions of moonlight, relative strengths, etc., again. I, for my part, will do my utmost to contribute to success.

"As for my health, I'm feeling quite on top of my form. There are such big things at stake. If our blow succeeds, it might go some way towards deciding the whole course of the war. If it fails, at least I hope to give the enemy a pretty thorough beating. Neurath has seen the Führer, who sent me his best wishes. He is fully aware of my anxieties."

At 0200 hours on the 31st, the Italo-German motorised column reached the first British minefield. The D.A.K., consisting of the tough 15th and 21st Panzer Divisions, was in the lead, followed by the Italian XX Corps, now commanded by General de Stefanis. Bringing up the rear was the 90th Light Division, which remained in close contact with the Italian X Corps, holding a pivotal position in the Axis line. All in all there were 515 tanks, of which 234 were German machines, including 26 of the new mark of Pzkw IV's mounting a 7.5-cm 43-calibre gun. The D.A.K. also had available 72 mobile 8.8-cm guns, but these were hardly used in an anti-tank role, because the 8th Army had learnt its lesson, and tanks were dug in as supplementary artillery.

Axis withdrawal

By 0300 hours on the 31st, it had dawned on Rommel that things were not going with their usual smoothness. Fired on by the guns of the 7th Armoured Division, and bombed by the Desert Air Force, some German tanks were coming up against unmarked minefields, whilst others were getting bogged down in bad going to the south of the Allied position. So that instead of making a push of 30-odd miles into the enemy's lines, the Axis mechanised forces had only covered about ten. Rommel would consequently have to give up the wheel he had intended to make after an initial deep push; but if he turned north now, he would come under fire from the crest of Alam el Halfa ridge, where XIII Corps, with 64 artillery batteries, 300 anti-tank guns, and the same number of tanks, was waiting.

Shortly afterwards, even worse news reached Rommel: Major-General Georg von Bismarck, commanding the 21st Panzer

Division, had been killed by a mine, and Lieutenant-General Walther Nehring, commanding the Afrika Korps, had been badly wounded in an air attack and replaced in the field by Colonel Bayerlein.

It was therefore no surprise that the D.A.K. attack on Hill 132, the highest point of the Alam el Halfa ridge, was repulsed; on its left, the Italian XX Corps fared no better — inevitably — in view of its light equipment; and the 90th Light Division, in the pivotal position, opposite the New Zealand Division, had its commander, Major-General Kleeman, seriously wounded in an air attack. The R.A.F., in fact, was everywhere, and on September 1 Rommel himself nearly met with the same fate as Nehring and Kleeman. Furthermore, despite the assurances showered on him by Cavallero and Kesselring, fuel supplies for the Panzerarmee were coming up more and more slowly. Accordingly, on the morning of September 3, Rommel took the decision to withdraw his troops.

First round to Montgomery

Preoccupied with his plans for a general offensive, Montgomery decided not to exploit this defensive success. It had cost the 8th Army 1,750 men and 67 tanks, whilst Axis losses were 536 dead, 1,760 wounded, and 569 missing, together with 49 tanks, 55 guns, and 395 trucks captured or destroyed. These are the figures for the battle of Alam el Halfa, which General Mellenthin has described as follows:

"8th Army had every reason to be satisfied with this victory, which destroyed our last hope of reaching the Nile, and revealed a great improvement in British tactical methods. Montgomery's

German MG34 machine gun in North Africa.

conduct of the battle can be assessed as a very able if cautious performance, in the best traditions of some of Wellington's victories."

The day after his victory, Montgomery wrote to a friend:

"My first encounter with Rommel was of great interest. Luckily I had time to tidy up the mess and to get my plans laid, so there was no difficulty in seeing him off. I feel that I have won the first game, when it was his service. Next time it will be my service, the score being one-love."

British Artillery fire on enemy positions in North Africa.

In his headquarters at Burg et Arab, Lieutenant-General Montgomery was carrying on with his preparations for Operation "Lightfoot", as G.H.Q. Cairo called the third British offensive in North Africa. First of all, in the light of experience gained at Alam el Halfa, Montgomery demanded new leaders for XXX Corps and the 7th Armoured Division. For the former he got Lieutenant-General Sir Oliver Leese, formerly commander of the Guards Armoured Division in Britain, and for the latter Major-General A. F. Harding. These were excellent choices, as can be seen from the later careers of these officers: Leese went on to command an army group in Burma and Harding became a Field-Marshal after the war.

One of Montgomery's early decisions was where to make his first attack. So far, Wavell, Rommel, and Auchinleck had all manoeuvred over the desert in order to drive the enemy into the Mediterranean. But by launching his attack in the northern sector, that is between Ruweisat Ridge and the sea, Montgomery thought that there was a good chance that Rommel would be surprised - provided, of course, that he still believed that Montgomery himself would stick to the tried and tested tactics used by his predecessors and the Germans. Also, if he moved in from the north, the desert in the south would play the same part as the sea in offering a complete obstacle in the event of a breakthrough. Originally Montgomery had stuck to the tactics laid down by the British and German military doctrine of the period: if the enemy's tanks could be knocked out at the beginning, his infantry was at your mercy. He was courageous enough to state that in open ground, given the training of their crews, the Panzers were more manoeuvrable than the British tanks and had a good chance of tearing them to pieces. Montgomery was also determined, if at all possible, to adhere to one of the most basic rules of desert war- fare. He had no intention of allowing his own tanks to attack Rommel's anti-tank guns, unless they were supported by Allied infantry.

So a change of method was needed and Montgomery has explained this perfectly clearly in his memoirs: "My modified plan now was to hold off, or contain, the enemy armour while we carried out a methodical destruction of the infantry divisions holding the defensive system. These un-armoured divisions would be destroyed by means of a 'crumbling' process, the enemy being attacked from the flank and the rear and cut off from their supplies. These operations would be carefully organised from a series of firm bases and would be within the capabilities of my troops."

Thus Rommel was due for a second surprise. Already deceived about the sector where the 8th Army would make its main thrust, he would also be caught out by his enemy's sudden change of tactics. It could be assumed that he would not remain inactive in face of the danger of seeing his divisions fall apart and then disintegrate. He could be expected to launch counter-attack after counterattack, but it would only be to find his Panzers deprived of all freedom of movement in the middle of the innumerable minefields protecting the British infantry positions and being fired on by the British armour, waiting steadfastly for them as they had done at Alam el Halfa.

The successful execution of this plan in which nothing was left to chance, required the organisation of a third corps, in addition to XIII and XXX Corps. This was to be X Corps, under the command of Lieutenant-General Herbert Lumsden. It consisted of armoured divisions and its job was to be the immediate exploitation of the infantry's advance along the line of the main thrust, then, once a breach was made, to pursue and destroy the enemy. Originally it was to have had the 1st, 8th, and 10th Armoured Divisions, but, to the great chagrin of its commander, Major-General C. H. Gairdner, the 8th had to be disbanded to make up the tank strength of the other two.

The headquarters and communications units played an equally important part in the execution and success of Operation "Bertram". This was the name given by the 8th Army to the deceptions carried out under Major Charles Richardson to convince the enemy that the threat of attack was increasing in the south. To this end the 8th Army used a large number of dummy vehicles, made of rubber and inflated by compressed air. No vehicle left the south for the northern sector without being replaced by a dummy. In the same sector Axis reconnaissance aircraft could watch the laying of a pipe-line, also a dummy, and calculate from the progress of the work that the expected attack would not start before November 1. Finally radio messages from the pseudo-8th Armoured Division made Panzerarmee H.Q. think that there was another armoured division between the Qattara Depression and the Ruweisat Ridge.

All this ingenuity would have been of little avail, however, if in the northern sector, where Montgomery was preparing to attack with seven divisions, the 8th Army's camouflage units had not successfully hidden from prying enemy aircraft the. thousands of vehicles and enormous storage depôts, and if the secret of Operation "Lightfoot" had not been jealously guarded. In fact, lower-ranking officers, N.C.O.s, and men were not informed of the date of the offensive until two days before the attack.

Parallel with this enormous effort of organisation, there was an intensive training programme for the troops by Montgomery, a first-class instructor. All this activity explains why, in spite of the Prime Minister's impatience, it was out of the question for the 8th Army to attack before the October full moon which was on the 23rd. We may therefore conclude that in once more tempering the ardour of Winston Churchill, General Sir Alan Brooke showed himself to be a truly great servant of his country and a major architect of her final victory.

German and Italian deployment

On the other side, Rommel had left Africa and handed over command of the Panzerarmee to General Georg Stumme, who had played an important part at the head of the XL Motorised Corps in Greece and then maintained his high reputation in Russia. This new posting relieved him of the disgrace into which he had fallen with the Führer as a consequence of his corps' operations orders falling into the hands of the Russians on the eve of Operation "Blau", Germany's 1942 Russian offensive. He had merely a holding role, however, and was not allowed to take much initiative, having to content himself with the programme left him by Rommel.

The armoured elements of the Panzerarmee had been withdrawn from the front as the force went over to the defensive. This left the Ramcke Brigade and five infantry divisions, including the German 164th Division and the Italian "Folgore" Airborne Division, in fixed defences. To the rear, in the northern sector, were the tough and mobile "Ariete" Armoured Division and 21st Panzer while in the southern sector were the 15th Panzer Division and the "Littorio" tank Division. In army reserve, the 90th Light Division and the "Trieste" Motorised Division were deployed in depth along the coastal road. Thus the 164th Division and two battalions of the Ramcke Brigade together with the Italian XXI Corps held the position where the enemy attack was expected, while two battalions of paratroopers were stationed with X Corps south of the Ruweisat Ridge.

The time taken to mount Operation "Lightfoot" was naturally not wasted by the Axis forces, which were deployed in depth and considerably strengthened. The units were contained within closed strongpoints protected by more than 445,000 mines, of which 14,000 were antipersonnel ones intended to discourage the enemy's engineers. Under the direction of Colonel Hecker, Rommel's chief of engineering, Italian and German engineers had also contrived booby traps of truly diabolical imagination, using even aeroplane bombs. These defences were naturally covered by machine guns and anti-tank guns. As regards the latter, on October 23, 1942 the D.A.K. had 86 8.8-cm weapons and 95 Russian 7.62-cm guns, of which 30 had been mounted on Czech

Shell explodes near observation post.

Italian self propelled guns at Carro Semovente.

tank chassis. The British considered these almost as deadly as the famous "88".

It was a hard nut to crack. But between the opposing shores of the Mediterranean, traffic conditions had not improved. Far from it, though Cavallero had thrown in everything he could get hold of. In September 40,465 tons of war matériel and 31,061 tons of petrol reached North Africa, 80 per cent of the supplies loaded in Italy. But in October losses rose to 44 per cent and the Axis forces opposing Montgomery got only 12,308 tons of liquid fuel. Cavallero asked Kesselring to put pressure on Malta; he replied by recalling some bomber squadrons from Libya. Although 300 twin-engined German bombers took part in this renewed offensive, it

was a total failure and the losses were so heavy that Göring, going over the head of Comando Supremo on October 20, ordered it to stop.

"Lightfoot" is launched

At 2140 hours on October 23, 1942, the El Alamein front lit up with a blaze of gunfire over its whole length. Between the sea and Ruweisat Ridge 456 guns opened fire to blast the way open for XXX Corps. In the south XIII Corps had 136 guns.

The attack was a complete surprise: at the time the battle started the commanders of the Italian XXI and X Corps (Generals Navarrini and Nebbia respectively) were on leave in Italy and only got back to their H.Q.s at the same time as Rommel. This was the curtain-raiser for 12 days of battle fought out between 12 Axis and 10 Allied divisions, though these numbers are misleading: Montgomery had the advantage in both men and matériel. In round numbers Montgomery deployed 195,000 men against some 50,000 Germans and 54,000 Italians.

The 8th Army's artillery barrage lasted 15 minutes. It effectively silenced the enemy's batteries and damaged his telephone communications and minefields, where many of the aircraft bombs were blown up. At 2200 hours the sappers advanced into no-man's-land, using the first mine-detectors to reach North Africa. Behind the sappers there were a small number of "Scorpion" tanks, special adaptations of ordinary tanks, designed to set off mines with whirling flails attached to a drum in front of the tank. Behind these followed the infantry, with fixed bayonets.

In the southern sector, XIII Corps (Sir Brian Horrocks), whose rôle was to put on a diversionary attack, had been ordered to hold back its 7th Armoured Division. The advance of its major infantry formations, 44th Division (Major-General I. T. P. Hughes) and 50th Division (Major-General J. S. Nichols) was consequently limited and secured at heavy cost against the determined resistance of the "Pavia" and "Brescia" Divisions and the paratroops of the "Folgore", commanded respectively by Generals Scattaglia, Brunetti, and Frattini. On the left flank, the 1st Fighting French Brigade confirmed its fighting spirit on the Qaret et Himeimat, but had to yield some of the ground it had won. Horrocks' objective had been achieved: to prevent the enemy from deploying the "Ariete" Armoured Division (General F. Arena) and the 21st

British guns firing at Germans El Alamein.

Panzer Division (Major-General von Randow) in support of the rest of the Axis forces in the northern sector.

The Axis infantry crumbles away

In the northern sector, XXX Corps' job was to make an inroad along two "corridors" in the minefields. The right-hand corridor was given to the 9th Australian

Division and the 51st (Highland) Division, newly arrived in North Africa and commanded by Major-General D. N. Wimberley; the left-hand corridor went to the New Zealand Division. None of these divisions reached the objectives marked for them on the map, but their action began the destruction of the enemy infantry, as foreseen by Montgomery. The "Trento" Division (General Masina) was very badly mauled and the 164th Division (Major-General Lungershausen) had two of its battalions virtually wiped out. But since the British infantry had failed to clear corridors right through the enemy minefields, the tanks of X Corps were jammed up in the enemy's defences. Montgomery ordered Lumsden to punch a way through but the attempt failed with considerable losses in men and machines. On the other side, General Stumme, who was roaming the battlefield alone, had a heart attack and fell from his vehicle without his driver noticing it. His death was a considerable blow to the Axis forces and his command was taken over in the evening of the 24th by the commander of the D.A.K., Lieutenant-General Ritter von Thoma.

On October 25 Montgomery ordered XIII and XXX Corps to press home their attacks. But they both failed to reach their objectives and so, with great coolness and resolution, Montgomery began to organise a fresh onslaught.

Rommel sees his danger

When he got back to his H.Q. in the even ing of October 26, Rommel realised exactly how serious the situation was. It had been saved only by the engagement of the 90th Light Division and the armoured group in the northern sector. Major-General von Vaerst's 15th Panzer Division had only 39 tanks left and General Bitossi's "Littorio" Armoured Division only 69. He therefore ordered the 21st Panzer Division with its 106 tanks to move north of Ruweisat Ridge. Once he had concentrated

Libya - British troops occupy Barce, a white flag flies over Fascist HQ.

his remaining armour Rommel tried to regain the initiative. He led the Axis tanks in a counter-stroke against the British penetrations. However, Montgomery's forces were ready to meet him. A heavy toll was taken of the Axis troops by bombers of the Desert Air Force and an anti-tank screen which contained many of the new 6-pounder anti-tank guns. Rommel was repulsed and this was a major success for Montgomery and the 8th Army. In XXX Corps, the 9th Australian Division struck north-west and trapped the 164th Division against the sea. The 1st South African Division (Major-General D. H. Pienaar) and the 4th Indian Division (Major-General F. I. S. Tuker), which formed Sir Oliver Leese's left flank, made a deep penetration into the positions of the "Bologna" Division (General Gloria). The struggle had now become a battle of attrition. And since the 8th Army had a massive numerical superiority, it had all the advantages in this type of struggle. On October 29 Rommel wrote to his wife: "The situation continues very grave. By the time this letter arrives, it will no doubt have been decided whether we can hold on or not. I haven't much hope. At night I lie with my eyes wide open, unable to sleep for the load that is on my shoulders. In the day I am dead tired. What will happen if things go wrong here? That is the thought that torments me day and night. I can see no way out if that happens."

However, Churchill could not contain his impatience at Montgomery's failure to break-through to win a swift success and summoned General Brooke to his office the same day. "What," he asked, "was my

Monty doing now, allowing the battle to peter out? (Monty

El Alamein - British troops pass an Italian M13-40 tank.

was always my Monty when he was out of favour.) He had done nothing now for the last three days and now he was withdrawing troops from the front. Why had he told us that he would be through in seven days if all he intended to do was to fight a half-hearted battle?"

Montgomery redoubles his efforts

As usual the Chief of the Imperial General Staff was able to placate Churchill and was well seconded in this by Field Marshal Smuts, who enjoyed the Prime Minister's special confidence. Montgomery had, in fact, withdrawn one brigade each from the 44th, 50th (XIII Corps), and 51st (XXX Corps) Divisions and given them to the New Zealand Division which, under Major-General Freyberg, was to be the spearhead of Operation "Supercharge" for the decisive breakthrough. Meanwhile XXX Corps had continued to hammer the enemy and forced Rommel to engage the "Ariete" Armoured Division and the "Trieste" Motorised Division, his last reserves.

"Supercharge" was being followed in London with some anxiety: "During the morning," Montgomery records, "I was visited at my Tactical H.Q. by Alexander and by Casey who was Minister of State in the Middle East. It was fairly clear to me that there had been consternation in Whitehall when I began to draw divisions into reserve on the 27th and 28th October, when I was getting ready for the final blow. Casey had been sent up to find out what was going on; Whitehall thought I was giving up, when in point of fact I was just about to win. I told him all about my plans and that I was certain of success; and de Guingand spoke to him very bluntly and told him to tell Whitehall not to bellyache."

"Supercharge", unleashed on November 2, gave rise to battles of a ferocity unheard of in this theatre. Italian antitank guns fired on British tanks at a range of 20 yards and General Freyberg's 9th Armoured Brigade was reported to have lost 70 out of the 94 tanks it had started with. At the end of the day, and in spite of repeated attacks by the Desert Air Force, what remained of the Axis army had managed to form the semblance of a front, but this was the end. Rommel was now aware that his forces had reached the limits of effective resistance. The Afrika Korps had only 35 tanks left. These were far too few to stop the 8th Army's advance.

Hitler orders the Afrika Korps to its destruction ...

Rommel drew his conclusions from the situation and ordered his troops to withdraw. The movement had just begun when, on November 3 at 1330 hours a message from Hitler, a Führerbefehl, reached him. It was drawn up in the following terms:

"To Field-Marshal Rommel,

"In the situation in which you find yourself there can be no other thought but to stand fast and throw every gun and every man into the battle. The utmost efforts are being made to help you. Your enemy, despite his superiority, must also be at the end of his strength. It would not be the first time in history that a strong will has triumphed over the bigger battalions. As to your troops, you can show them no other road than that to victory or death."

... and precipitates British victory at Alamein

As the disciplined soldier that he was Rommel cancelled his order and instructed his troops to hold their positions. Fortunately for Rommel, Montgomery failed to exploit the opportunity given to him by the Führerbefehl by driving swiftly on and surrounding the Axis troops. In the afternoon of November 4 the 8th Army made a breach 15 miles wide in the threadlike front of the enemy in the area of Tell et Aggaqir. The tanks of X Corps broke through, demolished the "Ariete" Armoured Division in spite of heroic resistance and captured the commander of the D. A. K., General von Thoma, as he leapt out of his blazing vehicle. The mechanised units of Rommel's Panzerarmee managed

Shell explodes by British truck carrying infantry.

New Zealand troops escorting German and Italian prisoners.

to escape to the west, just as a fresh order arrived from Berlin sanctioning a withdrawal westwards after all. The whole of the Italian infantry, however, (the "Trento", "Bologna", "Brescia", and "Pavia" Divisions) were left stranded, as were the "Folgore" Airborne Division and the headquarters of X Corps. 104,000 troops took part in this battle: the Axis powers lost 25,000 killed and wounded and 30,000 prisoners, including nine generals and 7,802 Germans. A thousand guns and 320 tanks were destroyed or captured by the victors. The Allies lost 13,560 men, of whom 4,610 were killed or missing; most of the missing turned out to be dead. 500 Axis tanks were put out of action and many of them were irreparable. At Alamein not only had Axis strength in

North Africa been broken for ever but so was Rommel's morale, so that not for a moment did he consider making another stand at Halfaya and El Agheila, as Comando Supremo ordered. This gave rise to new friction between the Axis partners which was to bear fruit in 1943.

The long retreat starts

El Alamein was over. Rommel now started on his long retreat to Tunis, followed steadily by Montgomery's 8th Army, that was to see the end of Axis power in Africa.

Chronology of World War II

	1938
March 11	Anschluss — German annexation of Austria.
September 29	Munich Agreement signed.
October 5	Germany occupies Sudetenland.

	1939
March 14	Slovakia declares its independence.
March 31	Britain and France give guarantee to Poland.
April 7	Italy invades Albania.
May 22	Germany and Italy sign Pact of Steel.
August 23	Molotov-Ribbentrop pact signed between Germany and the Soviet Union.
September 1	Germany invades Poland.
September 1	Britain and France declare war on Germany.
September 17	Soviet Union invades Poland.
November 30	Soviet Union at war with Finland.

	1940
March 12	War between Soviet Union and Finland ends.
April 9	Germany invades Norway and Denmark.
April 14	Allied troops land in Norway.
May 10	Fall Gelb, the offensive in the West, is launched by Germany.
May 10	Churchill becomes Prime Minister of Great Britain.
May 14	Dutch Army surrenders.
May 26	Beginning of evacuation of Dunkirk.
May 28	Belgium surrenders.
June 2	Allies withdraw from Norway.
June 4	Dunkirk evacuation complete.
June 10	Italy declares war on Britain and France.
June 14	Germans enter Paris.
June 21	Italy launches offensive against France.
June 22	France and Germany sign armistice.
June 24	France and Italy sign armistice.
July 3	Royal Navy attacks French fleet at Mers el Kebir.
July 10	Beginning of the Battle of Britain.
September 17	Operation Sealion (the invasion of England) postponed by Hitler.
September 21	Italy and Germany sign Tripartite Pact.
September 27	Japan signs Tripartite Pact.
November 20	Hungary signs Tripartite Pact.
November 22	Romania signs Tripartite Pact.
November 23	Slovakia signs Tripartite Pact.

	1941
January 19	British launch East African campaign offensive.
January 22	Australian troops take Tobruk.
February 6	British capture Benghazi.
February 11	Rommel arrives in Libya.

March 25	Yugoslavia signs Tripartite Pact.
March 27	Yugoslavia leaves Tripartite Pact after coup d'etat.
March 28	Successful British naval action against Italians off Cape Matapan.
April 6–8	Axis forces invade Yugoslavia and Greece.
April 11	U.S.A. extends its naval neutrality patrols.
April 13	Belgrade falls to Axis forces.
April 14	Yugoslav forces surrender.
April 22	Greek First Army surrenders at Metsovan Pass.
May 16	Italians surrender to British at Amba Alagi.
May 20	Germans land on Crete.
May 24	H.M.S. Hood sunk by Bismarck.
May 27	Bismarck sunk by Royal Navy.
June 1	British withdraw from Crete.
June 2	Germany launches Operation Barbarossa against the Soviet Union.
July 27	Japanese troops invade French Indo-China.
September 19	Germans capture Kiev.
September 28	Three-power Conference in Moscow.
December 6	Britain declares war on Finland, Hungary and Rumania.
December 7	Japanese attack Pearl Harbor.
December 8	U.S.A. and Britain declare war on Japan.
December 8	Japanese invade Malaya and Thailand.
December 11	Germany and Italy declare war on the U.S.A.
December 14	Japanese begin invasion of Burma.
December 25	Japanese take Hong Kong.
1942	
February 15	Japanese troops capture Singapore from British.
February 27	Battle of the Java Sea.
February 28	Japanese invade Java.
March 8	Japanese invade New Guinea.
March 17	General MacArthur appointed to command South-West Pacific.
April 9	U.S. troops surrender in Bataan.
April 16	George Cross awarded to Island of Malta by H.R.H. King George VI.
April 26	Anglo-Soviet Treaty signed.
May 6	Japanese take Corregidor.
May 7	Battle of the Coral Sea.
May 20	British troops withdraw from Burma.
May 26	Rommel's Afrika Korps attack British at Gazala.
May 30	Royal Air Force launches first thousand-bomber raid on Germany.
June 4	Battle of Midway.
June 21	Rommel's Afrika Korps take Tobruk.
July 1	Sevastopol taken by Germans.
July 1	First Battle of El Alamein.
August 7	U.S. troops land on Guadalcanal.
August 11	PEDESTAL convoy arrives in Malta.
August 19	Raid on Dieppe.

August 31	Battle of Alam Halfa.
October 24	Second Battle of El Alamein.
November 8	Operation TORCH landings in North Africa.
November 11	Germans and Italians occupy Vichy France.
November 27	French fleet scuttled at Toulon.
1943	
January 14–24	Allied Conference at Casablanca.
January 23	British troops take Tripoli.
February 2	Germans surrender at Stalingrad.
February 8	Red Army captures Kursk.
February 13	Chindits launch first operation into Burma.
February 19	Battle for the Kasserine Pass.
April 19	First Warsaw rising.
April 19	Bermuda Conference.
May 11–25	TRIDENT conference in Washington.
May 13	Axis forces surrender in North Africa.
May 16	Royal Air Force "Dambuster" raid on Mohne and Eder dams.
May 24	U-boats withdraw from North Atlantic.
July 5	Battle of Kursk.
July 10	Allies land in Sicily.
July 25	Mussolini resigns.
September 3	Allies land on Italian mainland.
September 8	Surrender of Italy announced.
September 9	Allies land at Salerno.
September 10	Germans occupy Rome and Northern Italy.
October 13	Italy declares war on Germany.
November 6	Red Army captures Kiev.
November	First Allied conference in Cairo. 23–26
November 28–December 1	Allied conference in Teheran.
December 3–7	Second Allied conference in Cairo.
December 24	General Eisenhower promoted to supreme commander for OVERLORD, the Normandy landings.
1944	
January 22	Allies land at Anzio.
January 27	Red Army raises Siege of Leningrad.
January 31	U.S. forces land on Marshall Islands.
February 1	Battle for Monte Cassino begins.
March 2	Second Chindit operation into Burma.
May 11	Fourth Battle of Monte Cassino.
June 4	U.S. troops enter Rome.
June 6	Operation OVERLORD — Allied landings in Normandy.
June 19	Battle of the Philippine Sea.
July 1	Breton Woods conference.
July 20	Failed attempt to assassinate Hitler — July Bomb plot.
August 1	Second Warsaw rising.
August 4	Allied troops enter Florence.

August 15	Operation DRAGOON — Allied landings in southern France.
August 25	Germans in Paris surrender.
September 4	British troops capture Antwerp.
September	OCTAGON — Allied conference at Quebec. 12–16
September 17	Operation MARKET GARDEN at Arnhem.
September 21	Dumbarton Oaks conference.
October 14	British enter Athens.
October 23	De Gaulle recognised by Britain and U.S.A. as head of French Provisional Government.
October 24	Battle of Leyte Gulf.
December 16	Germans launch campaign in the Ardennes.
1945	
January 4–13	Japanese Kamikaze planes sink 17 U.S. ships and damage 50 more.
January 14	Red Army advances into East Prussia.
January 17	Red Army takes Warsaw.
January 30–February 3	First ARGONAUT Allied conference at Malta.
February 4–11	Second ARGONAUT Allied conference at Malta.
February 6	Allies clear Colmar pocket.
February 19	U.S. forces land on Iwo Jima.
February 26	U.S. 9th Army reaches Rhine.
March 7	U.S. 3rd Army crosses Rhine at Remagen Bridge.
March 20	British capture Mandalay.
March 30	Red Army enters Austria.
April 1	U.S. First and Ninth Armies encircle the Ruhr.
April 1	U.S. forces land on Okinawa.
April 12	President Roosevelt dies and Truman becomes president.
April 13	Red Army takes Vienna.
April 25	U.S. and Soviet forces meet at Torgau.
April 28	Mussolini shot by partisans.
April 29	Germans sign surrender terms for troops in Italy.
April 30	Hitler commits suicide.
May 2	Red Army takes Berlin.
May 3	British enter Rangoon.
May 4	German forces in the Netherlands, northern Germany and Denmark surrender to General Montgomery on Luneburg Heath.
May 5	Germans in Norway surrender.
May 7	General Alfred Jodl signs unconditional surrender of Germany at Reims, to take effect on May 9.
May 8	Victory in Europe Day.
May 10	Red Army takes Prague.
July 17–August 2	Allied TERMINAL conference held in Potsdam.
July 26	Winston Churchill resigns after being defeated in the general election. Clement Attlee becomes Prime Minister of Great Britain.
August 6	Atomic bomb dropped on Hiroshima.
August 8	Soviet Union declares war on Japan.
August 9	Atomic bomb dropped on Nagasaki.
August 14	Unconditional surrender of Japanese forces announced by Emperor Hirohito.
August 15	Victory in Japan Day.
September 2	Japanese sign surrender aboard U.S.S. Missouri in Tokyo Bay.